HARCOURT SCIENCE

GEORGIA TEST PREPARATION

GRADE **2**

TEACHER'S EDITION

Harcourt School Publishers

Orlando • Boston • Dallas • Chicago • San Diego

www.harcourtschool.com

ISBN 0-15-332654-9

4 5 6 7 8 9 10 054 10 09 08 07 06 05

© Harcourt

Contents

© Harcourt

Unit A   Living Things Grow and Change

Chapter 1—Plants Grow and Change

Chapter 2—Animals Grow and Change

Chapter 3—People Grow and Change

Unit A Math Practice

© Harcourt

Unit B — Homes for Living Things

Unit C | Exploring Earth's Surface

Unit D   Space and Weather

Chapter 1—The Solar System

Chapter 2—Earth's Weather

Unit E   Exploring Matter

Chapter 1—Observing and Measuring Matter

Chapter 2—Changes in Matter

© Harcourt

Unit F   Energy in Motion

Chapter 1—Forces and Motion

Chapter 2—Hearing Sound

Harcourt Science Georgia Test Preparation
Overview

Using This Resource

The purpose of this practice book is to help you prepare students for success with the Georgia Statewide Assessment Test. The book contains practice tests in the same format as the Assessment materials. Use of these tests can build students' test-taking skills before the state test and other standardized tests are administered. And because the practice test items relate to Georgia content standards and benchmarks in reading, writing, and mathematics, the use of these practice tests can reinforce students' knowledge and skills in the curriculum areas that are assessed.

Description of Components

The *Georgia Test Preparation* has three parts—reading comprehension, writing practice, and math practice. In each of these areas, the content is drawn from the *Harcourt Science* Pupil Edition (PE). Items in all three areas of the *Test Preparation* are correlated to specific Georgia content standards and benchmarks. Following is a brief description of each component.

Daily Reading Comprehension

- A reading comprehension practice test is provided for each lesson in the Pupil Edition (PE) of *Harcourt Science,* Grade 2.

- Children first read a lesson in their textbooks; then they complete related items in their *Test Preparation* books.

- Each passage is used to test more than one objective.

- Each item includes a purpose statement, a question to answer, or a sentence to complete based on the passage read. Items may also relate to photographs, illustrations, or diagrams.

- Instead of having children mark their answers on the page, you may choose to duplicate the generic answer sheet found in the front of this book.

- Answers are marked on the test pages in nonreproducible blue, so you may copy the test pages and the answers will not duplicate. However, for easy scoring you may wish to make an answer key by using a copy of the answer sheet and filling in the correct answers.

Writing Practice

- A writing practice exercise is included for each chapter in *Harcourt Science,* Grade 2.

- Practice in writing about science is provided, using various forms of discourse—descriptive, expressive, informative, and persuasive.

- Each writing practice exercise provides a title, a situation, and a task.

- Included in the front matter of this booklet are scoring rubrics to help you evaluate each type of writing exercise.

Mathematics Practice

- A math practice test is provided for each chapter in *Harcourt Science,* Grade 2. A math review test is provided for each unit.

- Practice test items deal with chapter science concepts as well as math standards and benchmarks.

- Each item includes a question to answer or a sentence to complete.

- Instead of having children mark their answers on the page, you may choose to duplicate the generic answer sheet found in the front of this book.

- Answers are marked on the test pages in nonreproducible blue, so you may copy the test pages and the answers will not duplicate. However, for easy scoring you may wish to make an answer key by using a copy of the answer sheet and filling in the correct answers.

Description of Stanford 9 Components

Objectives Practice

In this section of the book, children are given the opportunity to work with all the objectives addressed on the science portion of the Stanford 9 Test. Children mark their answers by filling in the bubble under the correct answer on the practice page. This will help them develop the skills necessary for taking standardized tests. The answers for the objectives practice questions are provided in nonreproducible blue on the student pages.

Practice Test

Like the science portion of the Stanford 9 Test, the practice test contains 20 items. This test is designed to be taken at one time to give children practice in maintaining the concentration required by the Stanford 9 Test. Distribute the tests to children, and review directions and the sample questions to ensure children understand how to mark their answers. The answers for the practice test are provided in nonreproducible blue on the student pages.

A list of Stanford 9 objectives as well as additional information on using this component may be found on page xxv.

School-Home Connection

Families often are anxious about state tests and want to help students be successful when taking the tests. You may wish to send home pages from this book with students and encourage family members and students to work together to complete the practice exercises.

Georgia Reading Content Standards

The following Georgia Reading Content Standards for grade 2 are addressed in the reading comprehension portion of this practice book. Correlations to specific practice pages can be found on the following page.

Strand: Written Communication

15 Standard: Increases vocabulary to reflect a growing range of interests and knowledge.

18 Standard: Reads a variety of materials for information and pleasure.

21 Standard: Demonstrates an understanding of semantic relationships by using context clues, word meanings, and prior knowledge in reading. (Semantics—"Does it make sense?")

23 Standard: Integrates language structure (syntax), meaning clues (semantics), phonetic strategies, and sight vocabulary when reading orally and silently.

25 Standard: Recognizes EXPLICIT main ideas, details, sequence of events, and cause-effect relationships in fiction and nonfiction.

26 Standard: Recognizes IMPLICIT main ideas, details, sequence of events, and cause-effect relationships in fiction and nonfiction.

29 Standard: Draws conclusions, makes predictions, and comparisons.

30 Standard: Reads for understanding and rereads as needed for clarification, self-correction, and further comprehension.

31 Standard: Demonstrates comprehension when reading a variety of literary forms (e.g., fiction, nonfiction, poetry, and drama).

33 Standard: Uses knowledge of root words, prefixes, and suffixes in word recognition.

Georgia Correlations for Reading Practice

The following grade 2 Reading Standards are addressed on the reading comprehension pages of this practice book. In the notations, the letter stand for the related Unit, the first number for the related Chapter, and the second number for the item number in the practice pages.

Reading Standards	Unit-Chapter-Item Number
• **Standard 15:** Increases vocabulary to reflect a growing range of interests and knowledge. • **Standard 33:** Uses knowledge of root words, prefixes, and suffixes in word recognition.	A-1-6, A-2-6, A-3-11, A-3-16, B-1-1, B-2-2, B-2-10, C-1-9, C-2-4, C-2-8, C-2-10, D-1-2, D-1-6, D-2-1, D-2-9, E-1-1, E-1-8, E-1-11, E-2-8, E-2-10, E-2-11, E-2-12, F-1-3, F-2-1, F-2-4, F-2-7, F-2-11
• **Standard 18:** Reads a variety of materials for information and pleasure. • **Standard 30:** Reads for understanding and rereads as needed for clarification, self-correction, and further comprehension. • **Standard 31:** Demonstrates comprehension when reading a variety of literary forms (e.g., fiction, nonfiction, poetry, and drama).	A-1-4, A-1-5, A-2-1, A-3-1, B-1-17, B-2-1, C-1-1, C-2-5, D-1-1, D-1-7, D-2-1, E-1-13, F-1-1, F-2-1
• **Standard 21:** Demonstrates an understanding of semantic relationships by using context clues, word meanings, and prior knowledge in reading. (Semantics— "Does it make sense?") • **Standard 23:** Integrates language structure (syntax), meaning clues (semantics), phonetic strategies, and sight vocabulary when reading orally and silently.	A-1-6, A-3-11, A-3-16, B-2-2, B-2-10, C-1-9, C-2-4, D-1-11, D-2-9, E-1-1, E-1-8, E-1-11, E-2-8, E-2-10, E-2-11, E-2-12, F-1-3, F-2-1, F-2-4, F-2-7, F-2-11
• **Standard 25:** Recognizes EXPLICIT main ideas, details, sequence of events, and cause-effect relationships in fiction and nonfiction. • **Standard 26:** Recognizes IMPLICIT main ideas, details, sequence of events, and cause-effect relationships in fiction and nonfiction.	A-1-4, A-1-11, A-2-3, A-2-4, A-3-1, A-3-3, A-3-6, A-3-9, A-3-14, A-3-15, B-1-4, B-1-7, B-1-10, B-1-19, B-2-4, B-2-6, C-1-6, C-2-1, C-2-11, D-1-10, D-1-16, D-2-3, D-2-5, D-2-6, D-2-7, D-2-11, D-2-14, E-1-2, E-1-9, E-1-16, E-2-3, E-2-4, F-1-4, F-1-6, F-1-9, F-1-12, F-2-5, F-2-6, F-2-15, F-2-16
• **Standard 29:** Draws conclusions, makes predictions, and comparisons.	A-1-1, A-1-2, A-1-3, A-1-7, A-1-8, A-1-9, A-1-10, A-1-11, A-1-12, A-2-2, A-2-5, A-2-7, A-2-8, A-3-1, A-3-2, A-3-4, A-3-5, A-3-7, A-3-8, A-3-9, A-3-12, A-3-13, A-3-14, B-1-3, B-1-5, B-1-6, B-1-8, B-1-9, B-1-11, B-1-12, B-1-13, B-1-14, B-1-15, B-1-16, B-1-18, B-1-20, B-2-3, B-2-4, B-2-5, B-2-7, B-2-8, B-2-9, B-2-11, B-2-12, C-1-1, C-1-2, C-1-3, C-1-4, C-1-5, C-1-7, C-1-8, C-1-10, C-1-11, C-1-12, C-2-2, C-2-3, C-2-6, C-2-7, C-2-9, C-2-12, D-1-1, D-1-3, D-1-4, D-1-5, D-1-8, D-1-9, D-1-12, D-1-13, D-1-14, D-1-15, D-2-4, D-2-8, D-2-11, D-2-12, D-2-13, D-2-14, D-2-16, E-1-3, E-1-4, E-1-5, E-1-6, E-1-7, E-1-10, E-1-11, E-1-14, E-1-15, E-2-1, E-2-2, E-2-5, E-2-6, E-2-9, F-1-1, F-1-5, F-1-7, F-1-8, F-1-10, F-1-11, F-2-2, F-2-3, F-2-8, F-2-9, F-2-10, F-2-13, F-2-14

Georgia Writing Content Standards

The following Georgia Writing Content Standards for grade 2 are addressed in the writing portions of this practice book. Correlations to specific practice pages can be found on the following page.

Strand: Written Communication

36 Standard: Uses correct spelling for frequently used sight vocabulary.

37 Standard: Uses learned phonetic strategies to spell correctly.

40 Standard: Writes a minimum of three sentences about a topic.

42 Standard: Writes in a variety of genres to include correspondence (including writing letters and addressing envelopes).

43 Standard: Applies correct principles of grammar:
- Writes complete sentences
- Uses correct capital letters
- Uses correct punctuation
- Applies correct rules of usage and expression.

44 Standard: Communicates ideas by using the writing process:

PREWRITING
- Generates ideas

DRAFTING
- Focuses on topic
- Uses prewriting ideas to complete first draft

REVISING
- Expands use of descriptive words
- Improves sequence
- Adds variety of sentence types
- Organizes writing to include a clear beginning, middle and ending

EDITING
- Begins each sentence and proper noun with a capital letter
- Uses correct spelling
- Uses appropriate punctuation
- Uses complete sentences

PUBLISHING
- Shares writing with others.

Correlations for Writing Practice

The following grade 2 Writing Standards are addressed on the Writing Practice pages of this book. The notations indicate the pages on which each prompt is found.

Writing Standards	Pages
• **Standard 36:** Uses correct spelling for frequently used sight vocabulary. • **Standard 37:** Uses learned phonetic strategies to spell correctly.	4, 7, 12, 23, 27, 36, 40, 50, 55, 65, 69, 78, 83
• **Standard 42:** Writes in a variety of genres to include correspondence (including writing letters and addressing envelopes).	4, 7, 12, 23, 27, 36, 40, 50, 55, 65, 69, 78, 83
• **Standard 43:** Applies correct principles of grammar: • Writes complete sentences • Uses correct capital letters • Uses correct punctuation • Applies correct rules of usage and expression.	4, 7, 12, 23, 27, 36, 40, 50, 55, 65, 69, 78, 83
• **Standard 44:** Communicates ideas by using the writing process: PREWRITING • Generates ideas. DRAFTING • Focuses on topic. • Uses prewriting ideas to complete first draft. REVISING • Expands use of descriptive words • Improves sequence • Adds variety of sentence types • Organizes writing to include a clear beginning, middle and ending EDITING • Begins each sentence and proper noun with a capital letter • Uses correct spelling • Uses appropriate punctuation • Uses complete sentences PUBLISHING • Shares writing with others.	4, 7, 12, 23, 27, 36, 40, 50, 55, 65, 69, 78, 83

© Harcourt

Georgia Mathematics Content Standards

The following Standards from the Georgia Mathematics Content Standards for grade 2 are addressed in the mathematics portions of this practice book. Correlations to specific practice pages can be found on the following page.

Strand Whole Number Computation; Estimation; Whole Number Operations

1 Standard: Estimates appropriate sums and differences (see computational objectives).

34 Standard: Determines basic addition facts (sums to 20) and related subtraction facts by using strategies such as near doubles, making ten, and using known facts to determine unknown facts.

36 Standard: Recalls addition facts (sums to 20) and related subtraction facts presented orally, vertically, and horizontally (rewrite vertically).

37 Standard: Uses models such as base ten blocks and pictorial representations to explore adding and subtracting one- and two-digit numbers (without regrouping).

38 Standard: Adds combinations of 1- , 2- , and 3-digit numbers without and with regrouping. Subtracts 1- and 2-digit numbers from 2- and 3-digit numbers without regrouping. Include vertical and horizontal presentation with the horizontal rewritten vertically.

39 Standard: Uses concrete objects to explore combining equivalent sets and uses skip-counting as readiness for multiplication.

Strand Number Sense & Numeration; Fractions & Decimals

3 Standard: Relates fractions (halves, thirds, and fourths) to concrete and pictorial models and relates models to fractions.

13 Standard: Counts by ones, twos, fives, and tens up to 100; threes to 36; and fours to 48.

16 Standard: Relates whole numbers up to 999 to concrete and pictorial models, relates models to numbers and orally names numbers (e.g., 3 hundreds, 2 tens, 4 ones; three hundred twenty-four; or $300 + 20 + 4 = 324$).

17 Standard: Determines ordinal numbers through twelfth.

Strand Geometry & Spatial Sense; Measurement

6 Standard: Identifies the shapes (e.g., two triangles to make a rectangle) that can be put together to make a given shape.

7 Standard: Measures length using inches and centimeters and selects objects having given dimensions.

8 Standard: Selects appropriate customary or metric units of measurement: minute, hour, day, week, month, inch, foot, centimeter, meter, cup, quart, liter, pound, or kilogram.

9 Standard: Selects appropriate instrument for determining specified measurement of height, weight, capacity, time, and temperature.

10 Standard: Applies appropriate units to measure time (minutes, hours, days, weeks, months, years), tells time to five minutes, and determines elapsed time.

11 Standard: Determines weight/mass of objects in ounces, pounds, grams, or kilograms.

12 Standard: Explores estimation of quantities (both dry and liquid) and length using standard units including inches and centimeters.

Strand Patterns & Relationships; Algebra

19 Standard: Describes and compares areas of similar regions (smaller, larger, same).

20 Standard: Identifies geometric relationships (larger, largest, smaller, smallest, same size, same shape, same size and same shape, inside, outside, on left, and on right).

22 Standard: Uses appropriate symbols $(+, -, =, <, >)$.

24 Standard: Predicts and completes patterns such as those involving numbers, shapes, colors, and events.

25 Standard: Recognizes equivalent sets and nonequivalent sets.

26 Standard: Identifies numerical relations (greater than, less than, and equal to).

27 Standard: Organizes elements of sets according to given characteristics (shading, color, shape, size, design, and use).

Strand Problem Solving

29 Standard: Recognizes in a problem-solving situation that addition reflects combining elements of sets and that subtraction reflects taking away or comparing elements of sets.

31 Standard: Solves one- and two-step word problems related to appropriate second-grade objectives. Includes oral and written problems and problems with extraneous information as well as information from sources such as bar graphs and pictographs.

32 Standard: Constructs and interprets simple bar graphs and pictographs with up to five columns, using whole unit data.

Correlations for Mathematics Practice

The following standards are addressed in this practice book. In the notations, the letter stands for the Unit in the Pupil Edition; the number stands for the item number in the practice test.

Math Standards	Pages
Strand Whole Number Computation; Estimation; Whole Number Operations	A3, A5, A8, A11, A12, A13, A15, A16, A18, A19, B2, B3, B4, B5, B6, B8, B9, B10, B11, B12, B14, B16, B18, B19, C2, C5, C6, C8, C9, C10, C11, C12, C16, C18, C19, C20, D5, D8, D11, D12, D16, D17, D18, D19, E10, E11, E13, E14, E15, E19, F1, F5, F8, F11, F13, F15, F16
Strand Number Sense & Numeration; Fractions & Decimals	A2, A5, A7, A8, A10, A12, A13, A15, A16, B1, B2, B3, B4, B5, B6, B8, B9, B10, B11, B12, B14, B15, B16, B17, B18, B19, C2, C3, C5, C6, C7, C8, C9, C10, C11, C12, C16, C18, C19, C20, D1, D2, D3, D4, D5, D6, D8, D9, D11, D12, D13, D14, D16, D17, D18, D19, E6, E7, E9, E10, E12, E14, E15, E17, E18, E19, F1, F13, F15, F16
Strand Geometry & Spatial Sense; Measurement	A1, A2, A4, A6, A9, A10, A20, B7, B13, B20, C2, C4, C11, C15, C17, D1, D2, D3, D4, D6, D7, D10, D15, D16, D20, E1, E2, E3, E4, E6, E7, E8, E12, E16, E17, E18, E20, F2, F9, F10, F12, F14, F17, F19, F20
Strand Patterns & Relationships; Algebra	A1, A3, A6, A7, A10, A11, A12, A14, A16, A17, A19, B2, B5, B6, B7, B9, B10, B11, B12, C1, C4, C5, C6, C7, C10, C12, C13, C14, C15, C19, C20, D7, D11, D12, D15, D17, D18, D19, E3, E4, E5, E9, E11, E13, F1, F3, F4, F5, F6, F7, F9, F10, F11, F12, F15, F18, F19, F20
Strand Problem Solving	A2, A3, A5, A8, A11, A12, A13, A15, A16, A17, A18, A19, B1, B2, B3, B4, B5, B6, B7, B8, B9, B10, B11, B12, B14, B15, B16, B17, B18, B19, C1, C2, C3, C4, C5, C6, C7, C8, C9, C11, C12, C13, C14, C16, C18, C19, C20, D1, D2, D3, D4, D5, D7, D8, D9, D11, D12, D13, D14, D15, D16, D17, D18, D19, E3, E4, D5, E6, E7, E9, E10, E11, E12, E13, E14, E15, E17, E18, E19, F1, F3, F4, F5, F6, F7, F8, F9, F10, F11, F12, F13, F14, F15, F16, F18, F19, F20

Developmental Stage/Scoring Guidelines
for Grade 2

Stage 1: The Emerging Writer

- Little or no topic development, organization, and/or detail.
- Little awareness of audience or writing task.
- Errors in surface features prevent the reader from understanding the writer's message.

Stage 2: The Developing Writer

- Topic beginning to be developed. Response contains the beginning of an organization plan.
- Limited awareness of audience and/or task.
- Simple word choice and sentence patterns.
- Errors in surface features interfere with communication.

Stage 3: The Focusing Writer

- Topic clear even though development is incomplete. Plan apparent although ideas are loosely organized.
- Sense of audience and/or task.
- Minimal variety of vocabulary and sentence patterns.
- Errors in surface features interrupt the flow of communication.

Stage 4: The Experimenting Writer

- Topic clear and developed (development may be uneven). Clear plan with beginning, middle, and end (beginning and/or ending may be clumsy).

- Written for an audience.

- Experiments with language and sentence patterns. Word combinations and word choice may be novel.

- Errors in surface features may interrupt the flow of communication.

Stage 5: The Engaging Writer

- Topic well developed. Clear beginning, middle, and end. Organization sustains the writer's purpose.

- Engages the reader.

- Effective use of varied language and sentence patterns.

- Errors in surface features do not interfere with meaning.

Stage 6: The Extending Writer

- Topic fully elaborated with rich details. Organization sustains the writer's purpose and moves the reader through the piece.

- Engages and sustains the reader's interest.

- Creative and novel use of language and effective use of varied sentence patterns.

- Errors in surface features do not interfere with meaning.

Writing Practice
General Scoring Guide for Teachers

SCORE 4	The child completes all important components of the task and communicates ideas clearly.
	The child demonstrates in-depth understanding of the relevant concepts and/or processes.
	Where appropriate, the child shows how ideas are connected.
SCORE 3	The child completes most important components of the task and communicates clearly.
	The child demonstrates understanding of major concepts even though he or she overlooks or misunderstands some less important ideas or details.
SCORE 2	The child completes some important components of the task and communicates those clearly.
	The child demonstrates that there are gaps in his or her conceptual understanding.
SCORE 1	Child shows minimal understanding.
	Child addresses only small portion of the required task(s).
SCORE 0	Response totally incorrect or irrelevant.
BLANK	Blank/no response.

Writing Practice
General Scoring Guide for Children

SCORE POINT 4	• You follow all directions. • You finish all parts of the question. • You show that you completely understand what is asked for. • You show how ideas work together.
SCORE POINT 3	• You follow most of the directions. • You finish most parts of the question. • You show that you understand some of the question. • You may make a few little mistakes or have some or wrong ideas.
SCORE POINT 2	• You follow some of the directions. • You finish some parts of the question. • Your answer may not be complete. • You understand only parts of the question.
SCORE POINT 1	• You understand only a small part of the information asked for in the question. • You only answer a small part of the question.
SCORE POINT 0	• Your answer is completely wrong or has nothing to do with the question.
BLANK	• You did not give any answer at all.

© Harcourt

Reading Comprehension—Answer Sheet

Name _____   Date _____

Unit _____   Chapter _____

1. Ⓐ Ⓑ Ⓒ Ⓓ

2. Ⓐ Ⓑ Ⓒ Ⓓ

3. Ⓐ Ⓑ Ⓒ Ⓓ

4. Ⓐ Ⓑ Ⓒ Ⓓ

5. Ⓐ Ⓑ Ⓒ Ⓓ

6. Ⓐ Ⓑ Ⓒ Ⓓ

7. Ⓐ Ⓑ Ⓒ Ⓓ

8. Ⓐ Ⓑ Ⓒ Ⓓ

9. Ⓐ Ⓑ Ⓒ Ⓓ

10. Ⓐ Ⓑ Ⓒ Ⓓ

11. Ⓐ Ⓑ Ⓒ Ⓓ

12. Ⓐ Ⓑ Ⓒ Ⓓ

13. Ⓐ Ⓑ Ⓒ Ⓓ

14. Ⓐ Ⓑ Ⓒ Ⓓ

15. Ⓐ Ⓑ Ⓒ Ⓓ

16. Ⓐ Ⓑ Ⓒ Ⓓ

17. Ⓐ Ⓑ Ⓒ Ⓓ

18. Ⓐ Ⓑ Ⓒ Ⓓ

19. Ⓐ Ⓑ Ⓒ Ⓓ

20. Ⓐ Ⓑ Ⓒ Ⓓ

21. Ⓐ Ⓑ Ⓒ Ⓓ

22. Ⓐ Ⓑ Ⓒ Ⓓ

23. Ⓐ Ⓑ Ⓒ Ⓓ

24. Ⓐ Ⓑ Ⓒ Ⓓ

Math Practice—Answer Sheet

Name _____   Date _____

Unit _____   Chapter _____

1. (A) (B) (C) (D)   13. (A) (B) (C) (D)
2. (A) (B) (C) (D)   14. (A) (B) (C) (D)
3. (A) (B) (C) (D)   15. (A) (B) (C) (D)
4. (A) (B) (C) (D)
5. (A) (B) (C) (D)   16. (A) (B) (C) (D)
                            17. (A) (B) (C) (D)
6. (A) (B) (C) (D)   18. (A) (B) (C) (D)
7. (A) (B) (C) (D)   19. (A) (B) (C) (D)
8. (A) (B) (C) (D)   20. (A) (B) (C) (D)
9. (A) (B) (C) (D)
10. (A) (B) (C) (D)   21. (A) (B) (C) (D)
                            22. (A) (B) (C) (D)
11. (A) (B) (C) (D)   23. (A) (B) (C) (D)
12. (A) (B) (C) (D)   24. (A) (B) (C) (D)

TEACHER'S NOTES

Stanford 9 Contents

Objectives Practice

Process Skills

Life Science

Earth Science

Physical Science

© Harcourt

Description of Practice for Stanford 9 Books
Overview

The purpose of the Harcourt Science Practice for Stanford 9 books is to help you prepare children for success with the science portion of the Stanford 9 Test. This book contains objectives practice pages and a practice test, all in the format of the Stanford 9 materials. Use of these materials can build children's test-taking skills before the Stanford 9 and other tests are administered.

Objectives Practice Pages

In this section of the book, children are given the opportunity to work with all of the objectives addressed on the science portion of the Stanford 9 Test. These objectives have been divided into four sections: Process Skills, Life Science, Earth Science, and Physical Science.

The pace at which you use the practice items depends on your teaching style. You may want to use one of the following ideas or a combination of several ideas.

- Have children complete each page of practice items immediately after the concept is presented in class.

- Group appropriate practice pages and have children complete them at given intervals, such as at the end of each unit.

- Provide a block of time at the beginning of the second semester or just before district or state standardized tests are administered. Have children complete all the practice items at this time, then try the practice test.

For the objectives practice section of this book, as in the Stanford 9 Test, the teacher reads the questions to children. The teacher's script of questions starts on page xxvii. Children mark their answers by filling in the bubble under the correct answer on the practice page. This will help them develop the skills necessary for taking standardized tests.

The answers for the objectives practice questions are provided in non-reproducible blue on the student pages. You may wish to score these practice pages yourself, have children help you score them, or score them as part of a class discussion.

Practice Test

Like the science portion of the Stanford 9 Test, the practice test contains 20 items. It is designed to be taken at one time to give students practice in maintaining the concentration required by the Stanford 9 Test.

As in the Stanford 9 Test, the teacher reads the test questions to children. The teacher's script for the practice test is found on page xxx.

The answers for the practice test are provided in non-reproducible blue on the student answer pages.

Teachers' Questions

Be sure all desks are cleared and that each child has two soft-lead (No. 2) pencils and an eraser.

Sample Questions

Two sample questions are found on the first page of the Objectives Practice section and at the beginning of the Practice Test. The sample questions are the same on both pages. To help children with the sample questions,

SAY

A   Look at Sample A in the shaded box at the top of the page. Here you see pictures of three different habitats. You know that a cactus is a plant that grows in a desert habitat. Which picture shows a desert?

Yes, that's right. The space under the second picture has been filled in to show that it is the right answer. Does everyone understand how to do this activity?

B   Now look at Sample B in the next shaded box. These pictures show three parts of a tomato plant. Mark under the part that takes water and nutrients from the soil. Which space did you mark?

Yes, you should have marked the space under the third picture, to show that it is the right answer. Are there any questions?

Objective Practice

Page 91

1.   Now move to Row 1 below Sample B. Look at the chart. It shows animals grouped by where they live. Which animal belongs in Group A? Mark your answer.

2.   Look at Row 2. Look at the first picture in the row. It shows a chart that groups animals by how their young are born. Which animal belongs in Group B? Mark your answer.

3.   Now move down to Row 3. John wants to find out if salt water dissolves soap bubbles faster than fresh water does. Mark under the experiment that would best answer this question.

4.   Move to the last row. Ramona wants to know which plant will grow better, a plant that is not covered with a paper bag or a plant that is covered. Mark under the experiment that best answers this question.

Look at the next page.

Page 92

1.   Look at the first row on this page. The circle graph shows kinds of vegetables in a garden. Mark under the one that takes up most of the garden. Is it peas, carrots, or tomatoes?

2.   Look at Row 2. This circle graph shows the weather for one month. Which were there the fewest of, rainy days, sunny days, or cloudy days? Mark your answer.

© Harcourt

3. Look at Row 3. Which is making the softest sound? Is it the flute, the bass violin, or the trumpet? Mark your answer.

4. Look at the pictures in the next row. Mark under the graph that shows that Monday has the highest temperature.

5. In the next row you see a food chain. Mark under the plant or animal that eats the grass.

6. Look at the next row. Here is another food chain. Mark under the plant or animal that begins the food chain.

Turn the page.

Page 93

1. Look at Row 1 on this page. These pictures show how a chicken grows. Mark under the picture that shows what a chicken looks like as an adult.

2. Go to Row 2. Mark under the picture that shows what happens to an acorn as it grows.

3. Move down to the next row. These pictures show a frog growing. Mark under the picture that shows the way the frog grows.

4. Move down to Row 4. Which beak is best for making holes in trees? Mark your answer.

5. Look at the next row. The first picture shows a picture of a duck. Which body part helps it swim? Is it the wings, the feet, or the beak? Mark your answer.

6. Go to the last row. Here are the teeth of three animals. Which animal eats plants? Mark your answer.

Look at the next page.

Page 94

1. Look at the first row on this page. The first picture shows a pine tree. Next to the picture are different kinds of leaves. Mark under the leaf that belongs to the pine tree.

2. Move down to Row 2. Look at the plant in the first picture. Which plant is most like the plant in the first picture? Mark your answer.

3. Move down to Row 3. Look at the pictures in the row. Which animal is most like those in the first picture? Mark your answer.

4. Move down to the next row, Row 4. Look at the pictures in the row. Mark under the animal that is most like the animals in the first picture.

5. Go to Row 5. Which picture shows a living thing that needs to eat food to get energy to grow? Mark under your answer.

6. Move down to the last row. Which of these eats plants to get energy? Is it the wolf, the lion, or the horse? Mark your answer.

© Harcourt

Turn the page.

Page 95

1. Now look at the first row on this page. The first picture shows a place where an animal can live. Mark under the animal that could most easily stay warm in this cold tundra habitat.

2. Now move down to Row 2. The first picture in this row shows plants and animals living in the ocean. Which animal could not easily find food in the ocean? Mark your answer.

3. Move down to the next row. Which part of this plant makes the plant's food? Is it the leaves, the stem, or the roots? Mark your answer.

4. Now look at the next row. These pictures show three parts of a plant. Mark under the part that carries water and nutrients to other parts of the plant.

5. Look at Row 5. Here are three pictures that show shadows. Mark under the picture that shows that the sun is very low in the sky.

6. Move down to the last row. These pictures show shadows. Mark under the picture that shows that the sun seems to be directly over the tree.

Look at the next page.

Page 96

1. Look at the first row on this page. Which thermometer shows the most likely temperature of the water in this scene? Mark your answer.

2. Look at Row 2. Which thermometer shows the most likely temperature of the air in this scene? Mark your answer.

3. Move down to the next row. Here you see the teeth of three dinosaurs. Which was most likely a plant-eating dinosaur? Mark your answer.

4. In the next row, which dinosaur could easily reach the leaves at the tops of trees? Mark your answer.

5. Look at Row 5. These pictures show a boy letting go of a book. Which picture shows what would happen to the book if there were no pull of gravity on Earth? Would the book rise to the ceiling, fall to the floor, or stay at the same level? Mark your answer.

6. In the last row, which picture shows an object being moved by the pull of gravity? Is it the floating balloon, the sailboat, or the moving truck? Mark your answer.

Turn the page.

Page 97

1. Now look at the first row on this page, Row 1. Which picture shows water changing from a solid to a liquid? Mark your answer.

2. Go to Row 2. Which picture best shows that heat was taken away from liquid water? Mark your answer.

Sample Questions (continued)

3. Now move down to Row 3. Mark under the container that is holding a gas. Is it the bowl of pasta, the balloon filled with air, or the pitcher of water?

4. Move down to the next row. Which picture shows a liquid? Is it the water from the faucet, the toy truck, or the popcorn? Mark your answer.

5. Go to the next row. Which object needs the least amount of force to move it from one place to another? Mark your answer.

6. Look at the pictures in the last row. Mark under the object that will be pulled by a magnet.

STOP

Practice Test

Be sure all desks are cleared and that each child has two soft-lead (No. 2) pencils and an eraser.

Turn to page 98.

Review the sample questions using the directions on page vi.

1. Now move down to Row 1 below Sample B. These pictures show a frog growing. Mark under the picture that shows the way the frog grows.

2. Look at Row 2. The first picture in this row shows plants and animals living in the ocean. Which animal could not easily find food in the ocean? Mark under your answer.

3. Now move down to Row 3. John wants to find out if salt water dissolves soap bubbles faster than fresh water does. Mark under the experiment that would best answer this question.

4. Move to the last row. Look at the pictures in the row. Mark under the animal that is most like the animals in the first picture.

5. Look at the first row at the top of the next page. It shows a food chain. Mark under the plant or animal that begins the food chain.

6. Look at Row 6. Which beak is best for making holes in trees? Mark under your answer.

7. Look at Row 7. Which part of this plant makes the plant's food? Is it the leaves, the stem, or the roots? Mark your answer.

8. In the next row, mark under the container that is holding a gas. Is it the bowl of pasta, the balloon filled with air, or the pitcher of water?

9. Look at the next row. Which thermometer shows the most likely temperature of the air in this scene? Mark your answer.

10. Move down to the last row, Row 10. Which is making the softest sound? Is it the flute, the bass violin, or the trumpet? Mark your answer.

© Harcourt

Sample Questions (continued)

Now turn the page.

11. Look at Row 11. Here are three pictures that show shadows. Mark under the picture that shows that the sun is very low in the sky.

12. Go to Row 12. Look at the chart. It groups animals by how their young are born. Which animal belongs in Group B? Mark your answer.

13. Move down to the next row. Mark under the object that will be pulled by a magnet.

14. Move down to Row 14. Which picture shows an object being moved by the pull of gravity? Is it the floating balloon, the sailboat, or the moving truck? Mark your answer.

15. Look at the next row. The first picture shows a pine tree. Next to the picture are different kinds of leaves. Mark under the leaf that belongs to the pine tree.

16. Go to the last row. Which picture shows a living thing that needs to eat food to get energy to grow? Mark your answer.

17. Look at the first row on the next page. The circle graph shows the weather for one month. Which were there the fewest of, rainy days, sunny days, or cloudy days? Mark your answer.

18. Move down to Row 18. Which dinosaur could easily reach the leaves at the tops of trees? Mark your answer.

19. Move down to Row 19. Which picture best shows that heat was taken away from liquid water? Mark your answer.

20. Move down to the next row, Row 20. Look at the picture of the duck. Mark under the body part that helps it swim. Is it the wings, the feet, or the beak?

STOP

TEACHER'S NOTES

What Are Living and Nonliving Things?

Read pages A5 to A7 in your textbook. Then read each question that follows. Decide which is the best answer to each question. Mark the letter for that answer.

1. How are living things different from nonliving things?

   (A) Living things are tall. Nonliving things are short.

   (B) Living things are young. Nonliving things are old.

   (C) Living things need food, water, and air. Nonliving things do not.

   (D) Living things make noise. Nonliving things do not make noise.

2. Which is a living thing?

   (A) a rabbit

   (B) a pencil

   (C) a sled

   (D) a rock

3. Which is a nonliving thing?

   (A) a tree

   (B) a rosebush

   (C) a snake

   (D) a mountain

4. In this lesson, which of these is **NOT** a **FACT** about all living things?

   (A) Living things need food.

   (B) Living things need air.

   (C) Living things need light.

   (D) Living things need water.

© Harcourt

How Do Plants Grow and Change?

Read pages A9 to A13 in your textbook. Then read each question that follows. Decide which is the best answer to each question. Mark the letter for that answer.

5. Which is **NOT** a **FACT**?

   (A) Flowers make seeds.

   (B) Roots use light to make food for a plant.

   (C) Stems move water through a plant.

   (D) Leaves use nutrients to make food for a plant.

6. The word <u>seedling</u> in this lesson means —

   (A) a plant that has seeds

   (B) a tiny seed

   (C) a young plant

   (D) an old plant

7. What does a seed do when it germinates?

   (A) It falls from the plant.

   (B) It dries up.

   (C) It freezes.

   (D) It starts to grow.

8. Look at this plant. Where is the sunlight coming from?

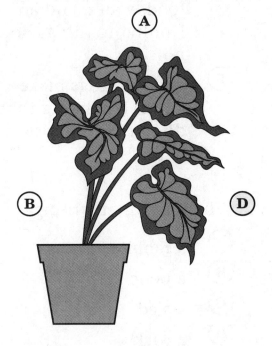

© Harcourt

How Are Plants Alike and Different?

Read pages A15 to A17 in your textbook. Then read each question that follows. Decide which is the best answer to each question. Mark the letter for that answer.

9. A pine tree's leaves look like —

   (A) stars

   (B) acorns

   (C) eggs

   (D) needles

10. Where do acorns grow?

   (A) on oak trees

   (B) on pine trees

   (C) on maple trees

   (D) on cactuses

11. What is this lesson **MOSTLY** about?

   (A) Plants grow in the desert.

   (B) Plants are different from one another.

   (C) A pine cone protects its small, hard seeds.

   (D) A cactus plant grows flowers.

12. Why is a cactus able to live in the desert?

   (A) It doesn't need water.

   (B) Its flowers act like little umbrellas to protect it from the sun.

   (C) Its flowers have a lot of water.

   (D) It has very thick stems that store water.

© Harcourt

Plant Parts

Plants have different parts, such as roots, stems, leaves, and flowers. Each part of a plant has a special job to do.

Pick a plant part (root, stems, leaves, flowers). Write a description of what that part looks like and what special job it does.

_____

_____

_____

_____

_____

_____

_____

_____

_____

_____

_____

_____

© Harcourt

How Are Animals Alike and Different?

Read pages A25 to A29 in your textbook. Then read each question that follows. Decide which is the best answer to each question. Mark the letter for that answer.

1. What is the **MOST** important idea of the paragraph on page A25?

   (A) Some animals have fur.

   (B) Animals use special body parts to fly.

   (C) There are many different kinds of animals.

   (D) All animals have some kind of body covering.

2. Mammals have —

   (A) feathers

   (B) smooth, wet skin

   (C) gills

   (D) fur or hair

3. Which is **NOT** a reptile?

   (A) a frog

   (B) a lizard

   (C) a turtle

   (D) a snake

4. Which animal does **NOT** have bones?

   (A) a chameleon

   (B) a turtle

   (C) a spider

   (D) a giraffe

What Are Some Animal Life Cycles?

Read pages A31 to A35 in your textbook. Then read each question that follows. Decide which is the best answer to each question. Mark the letter for that answer.

5. Which of these happens second?

Ⓐ A chick grows inside an egg.

Ⓑ The chick gets too big for the egg.

Ⓒ A bird lays an egg.

Ⓓ The chick breaks the eggshell and hatches.

6. A <u>veterinarian</u> is a doctor for —

Ⓐ children

Ⓑ very old people

Ⓒ teeth

Ⓓ animals

7. Which sentence is **NOT** true?

Ⓐ Most bird parents take care of their chicks.

Ⓑ Goslings are baby geese.

Ⓒ Baby robins can take care of themselves as soon as they are born.

Ⓓ Baby robins get new feathers as they become adults.

8. Which set of arrows shows a cycle?

Ⓐ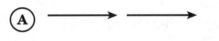

Ⓑ

Ⓒ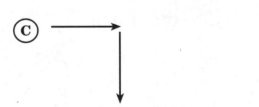

Ⓓ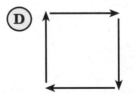

© Harcourt

Name _____

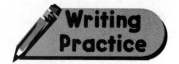

Animals with Bones

There are two groups of animals, those that have bones, and those that do not. There are many different kinds of animals that have bones.

Make a list of different kinds of animals that have bones. Write a sentence or two about each.

_____

_____

_____

_____

_____

_____

_____

_____

_____

_____

_____

_____

_____

_____

_____

© Harcourt

How Will I Grow?

Read pages A43 to A47 in your textbook. Then read each question that follows. Decide which is the best answer to each question. Mark the letter for that answer.

1. Which of these is **NOT** a FACT?

   Ⓐ When you are an adult, your body doesn't change.

   Ⓑ All people grow and change.

   Ⓒ As you get older, your skin will get wrinkles.

   Ⓓ Learning is a way to grow and change.

2. What are permanent teeth?

   Ⓐ teeth that grow in after your baby teeth fall out

   Ⓑ your two front top teeth

   Ⓒ the teeth that fall out

   Ⓓ a third set of teeth

3. Look at page A44. Which is the main idea on the page?

   Ⓐ First, you were a baby.

   Ⓑ Later on, you will be a teenager.

   Ⓒ All people grow and change.

   Ⓓ After that, you will become an adult.

4. Who is the oldest member of the family?

   Ⓐ the 15-year-old son

   Ⓑ the mother

   Ⓒ the father

   Ⓓ the grandmother

What Do My Bones and Muscles Do?

Read pages A49 to A53 in your textbook. Then read each question that follows. Decide which is the best answer to each question. Mark the letter for that answer.

5. Which one is a muscle?

   (A) the spine

   (B) the ribs

   (C) the skull

   (D) the heart

6. Which of these is **NOT** true about muscles?

   (A) Your muscles are under your skin.

   (B) Your muscles work in pairs.

   (C) Your muscles move your bones.

   (D) Your muscles hold up your body and gives it shape.

7. Which of these bones protect your heart?

   (A) ribs

   (B) leg bones

   (C) arm bones

   (D) foot bones

8. What is your skeleton?

   (A) the bones that help you move

   (B) the bones that protect parts inside your body

   (C) all of your bones

   (D) the part of the body that protects your bones

How Do My Heart and Lungs Work?

Read pages A55 to A59 in your textbook. Then read each question that follows. Decide which is the best answer to each question. Mark the letter for that answer.

9. Which sentence is **TRUE**?

   Ⓐ Your heart looks like your fist.

   Ⓑ Your heart acts like a fist.

   Ⓒ Your heart is about the same size as your fist.

   Ⓓ Everyone's heart is the same size.

10. What happens after air moves down to your lungs?

    Ⓐ Your heart pumps blood to all parts of your body.

    Ⓑ Your blood picks up oxygen from your lungs.

    Ⓒ Your blood takes the oxygen to your heart.

    Ⓓ Your lungs take in oxygen from the air.

11. <u>Rate</u> in this lesson means —

    Ⓐ size

    Ⓑ shape

    Ⓒ speed

    Ⓓ sound

12. What happens when you breathe in?

    Ⓐ Your lungs get larger.

    Ⓑ Your lungs get smaller.

    Ⓒ Your heart beats faster.

    Ⓓ Your heart slows down.

© Harcourt

How Do I Digest Food?

Read pages A61 to A65 in your textbook. Then read each question that follows. Decide which is the best answer to each question. Mark the letter for that answer.

13. The small intestine is connected to the —

   (A) stomach and large intestine

   (B) only the large intestine

   (C) only the stomach

   (D) stomach and the tube to the stomach

14. Which foods should you eat the **LEAST** of?

   (A) milk, yogurt, and cheese

   (B) meat and eggs

   (C) fats, oils, and sweets

   (D) dry beans and nuts

15. Which of these is **NOT** a group in the Food Guide Pyramid?

   (A) milk, yogurt, and cheese

   (B) fruits

   (C) bread, cereal, rice, and pasta

   (D) pizza, popcorn, and snacks

16. In this selection, <u>saliva</u> means —

   (A) the mouth

   (B) a bag of muscles that squeeze food

   (C) the liquid in your mouth that begins to break down food

   (D) the liquid food that moves into the small intestine

© Harcourt

Growth and Change

Every day, you learn more information and how to do more things. The information and skills you learn help you to grow and change.

Write a story about something you've learned. Explain when and how you learned whatever it was, and how it has helped you.

_____

_____

_____

_____

_____

_____

_____

_____

_____

_____

_____

_____

_____

_____

_____

© Harcourt

Unit A, Chapter 1

Math Practice

Choose the best answer. Mark the letter for that answer.

1. Jo planted an orange seed. About how long will it take for the seed to germinate?

   (A) more than 1 hour

   (B) less than 1 hour

2. How long is the pine needle? Mark your answer.

   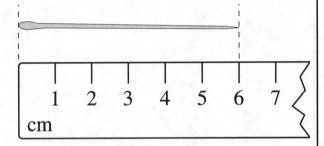

   (A) 4 centimeters

   (B) 5 centimeters

   (C) 6 centimeters

   (D) 7 centimeters

3. Mary has 5 walnuts and 3 pecans. Which number sentence shows how many nuts Mary has in all?

   (A) $5 - 3 = 2$

   (B) $3 + 2 = 5$

   (C) $3 \times 5 = 15$

   (D) $5 + 3 = 8$

4. Which tool should you use to measure the length of a leaf?

   (A)

   (B)

   (C)

   (D)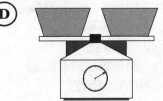

© Harcourt

Unit A, Chapter 2

Choose the best answer. Mark the letter for that answer.

5. Which graph best shows the information in the tally table?

KINDS OF PETS

Pet	Number of Pets
Mammal	II
Bird	II
Reptile	II
Amphibian	IIII
Fish	III

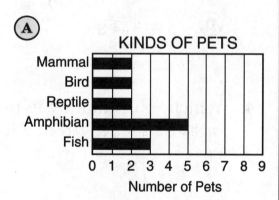

(A) KINDS OF PETS

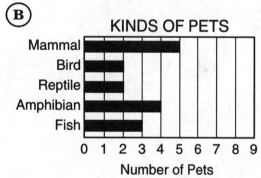

(B) KINDS OF PETS

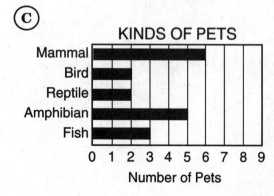

(C) KINDS OF PETS

6. About how much does an adult cat weigh?

(A) more than a pound

(B) less than a pound

7. Which insect is missing in the pattern?

(A)

(B)

(C)

8. Carlos saw 5 snakes and 9 alligators at the zoo. How many reptiles did he see in all?

(A) 11 reptiles

(B) 13 reptiles

(C) 14 reptiles

(D) 15 reptiles

© Harcourt

Unit A, Chapter 3

Choose the best answer. Mark the letter for that answer.

9. The clock shows Andy that it is time for dinner. What time does the clock show?

   (A) 5:15
   (B) 5:30
   (C) 5:45
   (D) 6:45

10. The spinner can stop on the heart, the lungs, or the skeleton. Which do you think it will stop on **MOST** often?

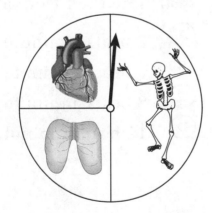

(A)   (C)

(B)

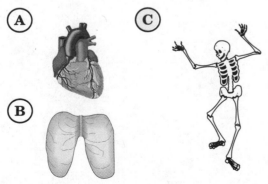

11. Tasha had 20 baby teeth. This year she lost 3 of them. Which shows how many baby teeth she has now?

   (A) $20 + 3 = 23$
   (B) $20 - 3 = 17$
   (C) $17 + 2 = 19$
   (D) $17 - 3 = 14$

12. Use the graph to answer the question below.

FAVORITE EXERCISE

Exercise	Number of Children
Playing Sports	👤👤👤👤
Swimming	👤
Running	👤👤👤
Walking	👤👤

Each 👤 stands for 2 children.

How many children like playing sports the best?

   (A) 2 children
   (B) 3 children
   (C) 4 children
   (D) 8 children

Go On

© Harcourt

Math Practice

Unit A, Chapter 3

Choose the best answer. Mark the letter for that answer.

13. There are 10 ladybugs on each of 3 leaves. There are 5 ladybugs on the ground. How many ladybugs are there in all?

Tens	Ones

(A) 13   (C) 35
(B) 15   (D) 53

14. Which items are in order from lightest to heaviest?

(A)

(B)

(C)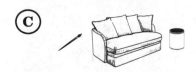

(D)

15. An ant has 3 body parts and 6 legs. How many legs do 3 ants have?

(A) 6 legs
(B) 9 legs
(C) 12 legs
(D) 18 legs

16. Donna's heart beats 62 times in a minute. Karen's heart beats 70 times in a minute. How much faster is Karen's heart rate than Donna's?

(A) 2 beats a minute faster
(B) 7 beats a minute faster
(C) 8 beats a minute faster
(D) 12 beats a minute faster

Stop

Unit A, Review

Choose the best answer. Mark the letter for that answer.

17. How does your heart rate change when you exercise?

Ⓐ Your heart rate gets faster.

Ⓑ Your heart rate gets slower.

Ⓒ Your heart rate stays the same.

18. Your wrist, palm, and fingers are part of your hand. There are 8 bones in your wrist, 5 bones in your palm, and 14 bones in your fingers. How many bones are in your hand?

Ⓐ 19 bones

Ⓑ 22 bones

Ⓒ 26 bones

Ⓓ 27 bones

19. Patrick traces his shoe and his father's shoe. Patrick's shoe is 8 inches long. His father's shoe is 14 inches long. Which number sentence shows how much longer Patrick's father's shoe is than his own shoe?

Ⓐ $14 - 8 = 6$

Ⓑ $14 - 6 = 8$

Ⓒ $8 + 6 = 14$

Ⓓ $8 - 6 = 2$

20. Which tool should you use to measure the length of a person's hand?

Ⓐ

Ⓑ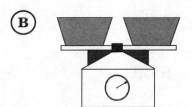

Ⓒ   Ⓓ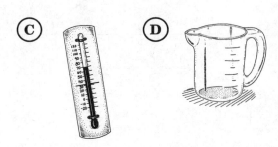

What Is a Habitat?

Read pages B5 to B7 in your textbook. Then read each question that follows. Decide which is the best answer to each question. Mark the letter for that answer.

1. In this lesson, <u>habitat</u> means —

    (A) all living and nonliving things in a place

    (B) a place where an animal finds the food, water, and shelter it needs to live

    (C) a cold environment

    (D) a forest

2. Which of these is an example of a habitat?

    (A) a sea otter

    (B) a fish

    (C) a tree

    (D) food

3. Look at the picture of the grebe on page B7. What is a grebe?

    (A) a small mammal

    (B) a fish

    (C) a bird

    (D) an insect

4. Which of these is NOT a FACT from the lesson?

    (A) Cougars eat fish.

    (B) An environment may have many different habitats.

    (C) Pelicans live by the ocean.

    (D) Caribou live in a cold environment.

What Are Different Land Habitats?

Read pages B9 to B13 in your textbook. Then read each question that follows. Decide which is the best answer to each question. Mark the letter for that answer.

5. Which habitat has plants that have to store water?

   Ⓐ a desert

   Ⓑ the rain forest

   Ⓒ the forest

   Ⓓ the tundra

6. Why aren't there any trees in the tundra?

   Ⓐ It is a cold and windy environment.

   Ⓑ There is too much snow.

   Ⓒ The summer is too short.

   Ⓓ There isn't enough water.

7. Which animal does NOT need a habitat that has trees?

   Ⓐ a raccoon

   Ⓑ a woodpecker

   Ⓒ a leaf bat

   Ⓓ a Gila monster

8. An emerald is a stone that is used to make jewelry. Look at the picture of the emerald tree boa on page B11. What color is an emerald?

   Ⓐ red

   Ⓑ green

   Ⓒ white

   Ⓓ blue

What Are Different Water Habitats?

Read pages B15 to B19 in your textbook. Then read each question that follows. Decide which is the best answer to each question. Mark the letter for that answer.

9. The bank of a pond is —

    Ⓐ a place to keep money

    Ⓑ the ground around the edge of a pond

    Ⓒ the bottom of a pond

    Ⓓ the surface of a pond

10. What is one way a pond is different from an ocean?

    Ⓐ A pond is a habitat. An ocean is not.

    Ⓑ A pond has fresh water. An ocean has salt water.

    Ⓒ A pond has plants. There are no plants in an ocean.

    Ⓓ An ocean has fish. A pond has only birds.

11. Which of these lives in a saltwater habitat?

    Ⓐ an otter

    Ⓑ a frog

    Ⓒ a muskrat

    Ⓓ a whale

12. A dolphin must come to the surface to —

    Ⓐ breathe air

    Ⓑ eat algae

    Ⓒ get sunlight

    Ⓓ find fish

© Harcourt

Unit B • Chapter 1 • Use with Lesson 3.

What Are Some Animal Adaptations?

Read pages B21 to B27 in your textbook. Then read each question that follows. Decide which is the best answer to each question. Mark the letter for that answer.

13. An animal that spends the winter in a deep sleep is —

Ⓐ estivating

Ⓑ hibernating

Ⓒ migrating

Ⓓ camouflaging

14. Animals migrate to —

Ⓐ find food

Ⓑ have young

Ⓒ neither of these

Ⓓ both of these

15. During estivation, an animal does not need —

Ⓐ sleep

Ⓑ protection

Ⓒ food or water

Ⓓ shelter

16. Camouflage is an adaptation that gives animals —

Ⓐ protection

Ⓑ food

Ⓒ warmth

Ⓓ sleep

© Harcourt

How Do Plants and Animals Help Each Other?

Read pages B29 to B33 in your textbook. Then read each question that follows. Decide which is the best answer to each question. Mark the letter for that answer.

17. Which sentence tells the most important idea of the paragraph on page B29?

   (A) Bees and flowers help each other.

   (B) Nectar is a sweet liquid.

   (C) Bees eat nectar.

   (D) Flowers make seeds.

18. What is one way animals help plants?

   (A) Birds spread seeds of the berries they eat.

   (B) Pandas eat the leaves and stems of bamboo.

   (C) Raccoons live in hollow trees.

   (D) Birds use twigs and dead leaves to make their nests.

19. These sentences tell what happens in one food chain. Which sentence happens last?

   (A) Plants grow on the surface of a pond.

   (B) A fish eats water beetles.

   (C) A blue heron eats a fish.

   (D) Water beetles eat the pond plants.

20. What is one way plants help animals?

   (A) Seeds stick to an animal's fur.

   (B) Plants provide seeds and fruits for birds to eat.

   (C) Animals move seeds to new places.

   (D) Seeds fall to the ground and may germinate.

© Harcourt

Name _____

Water Environment

There are many different environments on Earth. They are divided into land environments and water environments.

Choose a water environment. Write a paragraph telling about this environment. Be sure to include information on the plants and animals living there.

_____

_____

_____

_____

_____

_____

_____

_____

_____

_____

_____

_____

_____

_____

© Harcourt

How Does Weather Change Habitats?

Read pages B41 to B45 in your textbook. Then read each question that follows. Decide which is the best answer to each question. Mark the letter for that answer.

1. Which of these is **NOT** a FACT from the lesson?

   (A) Without enough water, most pond plants die.

   (B) When it floods, plants and animals get too much water.

   (C) A pond can dry up in a drought.

   (D) Lightning can cause floods.

2. A drought is —

   (A) a time with a lot of rain

   (B) a long time without rain

   (C) a time with some rain

   (D) a time with rain, snow, and ice

3. When lightning strikes a tree in a forest, it may catch fire if —

   (A) there are many trees in the forest

   (B) the forest has had too much rain

   (C) the forest is dry

   (D) there are many small plants in the forest

4. What happens after a fire burns a forest?

   (A) Slowly, the forest begins to regrow.

   (B) The forest dies completely.

   (C) The forest slowly turns into a pond.

   (D) Animals never return.

© Harcourt

How Does Pollution Change Environments?

Read pages B47 to B51 in your textbook. Then read each question that follows. Decide which is the best answer to each question. Mark the letter for that answer.

5. What is waste that harms land, water, or air called?

   (A) endangered

   (B) trash

   (C) litter

   (D) pollution

6. What is the main idea of the paragraph on page B50?

   (A) All living things need clean, unpolluted water.

   (B) Pollution is bad.

   (C) Rivers, lakes, and streams can be affected by water pollution.

   (D) Pollution changes water habitats.

7. The sea turtle is —

   (A) endangered

   (B) plentiful

   (C) in no danger from water pollution

   (D) a source of pollution

8. Which of the following causes air pollution?

   (A) litter

   (B) waste from farms

   (C) endangered animals

   (D) factories that produce smoke and fumes

How Do People Help the Environment?

Read pages B53 to B57 in your textbook. Then read each question that follows. Decide which is the best answer to each question. Mark the letter for that answer.

9. All of these people are going to the supermarket. Who is polluting the air on the way?

Ⓐ Martha is riding her bicycle.

Ⓑ David is skating.

Ⓒ Mr. Edwards is driving his car.

Ⓓ Mrs. Jackson is walking.

10. In this lesson, <u>reuse</u> means to —

Ⓐ not use

Ⓑ use again

Ⓒ throw away

Ⓓ make larger

11. Look at the picture on B55. Which symbol shows that the trash in this plastic bin is for recycling?

Ⓐ

Ⓑ

Ⓒ

Ⓓ

12. One way people take care of water is by —

Ⓐ planting trees

Ⓑ making less trash

Ⓒ recycling

Ⓓ not putting waste into it

© Harcourt

Name _____

Helping the Environment

People can help to keep the environment clean. There are several different ways to do this.

Think about ways you can help to keep the environment clean. Make a list of things you can do to help out. From your list, write a paragraph showing how you can help the environment.

_____

_____

_____

_____

_____

_____

_____

_____

_____

_____

_____

© Harcourt

Unit B, Chapter 1

Choose the best answer. Mark the letter for that answer.

1. It is warm in the forest in the summer. What is the temperature? Mark your answer.

   Ⓐ 70°F
   Ⓑ 75°F
   Ⓒ 80°F
   Ⓓ 85°F

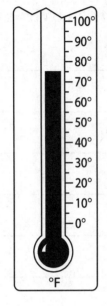

2. Which animal did the fewest children see at the pond? Mark your answer.

   POND ANIMALS

Animals	Number of Children
Otter	‖
Turtle	卌
Snake	‖‖
Duck	卌 ‖

   Ⓐ otter
   Ⓑ turtle
   Ⓒ snake
   Ⓓ duck

3. There are 4 polar bears living in the tundra. Each polar bear eats 4 fish. How many fish do they eat in all? Mark your answer.

   Ⓐ 12
   Ⓑ 14
   Ⓒ 16
   Ⓓ 18

4. A pelican ate 9 fish on Friday and 6 fish on Saturday. How many fish did the pelican eat in all? Mark your answer.

   Ⓐ 13
   Ⓑ 14
   Ⓒ 15
   Ⓓ 16

© Harcourt

Go On

Unit B, Chapter 1

Choose the best answer. Mark the letter for that answer.

Use the graph to answer Questions 5 and 6.

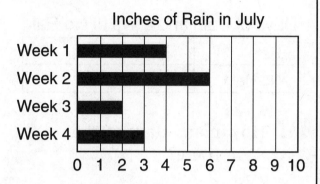

Inches of Rain in July

5. How many inches of rain fell in Week 1?

Ⓐ 3 inches

Ⓑ 4 inches

Ⓒ 6 inches

Ⓓ 8 inches

6. Which week had two more inches of rain than Week 1?

Ⓐ Week 1

Ⓑ Week 2

Ⓒ Week 3

Ⓓ Week 4

7. Paul sat by the ocean and saw the sunrise at

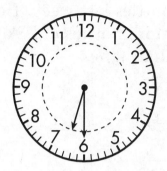

He ate breakfast 2 hours later. What time did he eat breakfast?

Ⓐ 7:30

Ⓑ 8:00

Ⓒ 8:30

Ⓓ 9:00

8. There were 25 birds in a tree in a rain forest. Then 32 more birds came. How many birds in all were in the tree?

Ⓐ 7

Ⓑ 57

Ⓒ 157

Ⓓ 570

Unit B, Chapter 2

Choose the best answer. Mark the letter for that answer.

9. Jane recycled 10 bottles last week. Skip recycled 15 bottles last week. How many more bottles did Skip recycle than Jane?

(A) 5

(B) 15

(C) 20

(D) 25

10. Yesterday 2 inches of snow fell. Today 4 inches of snow fell. Which number sentence shows how many inches of snow fell in all?

(A) $4 - 2 = 2$

(B) $2 + 2 = 4$

(C) $6 - 4 = 2$

(D) $2 + 4 = 6$

Use the tally table to answer Questions 11 and 12.

Days of Rain and Days of No Rain

Rain	卌 I
No Rain	IIII

11. How many days of rain were there?

(A) 3

(B) 4

(C) 5

(D) 6

12. How many more days of rain than days of no rain were there?

(A) 1

(B) 2

(C) 3

(D) 4

Go On

Unit B, Chapter 2

Choose the best answer. Mark the letter for that answer.

13. Which tool should you use to measure the amount of water in a pail?

    (A)

    (B)

    (C)

    (D)

14. Pat has 15 sheets of paper to recycle. Jack has 17 sheets of paper to recycle. How many sheets of paper in all do they have to recycle?

    (A) 12
    (B) 22
    (C) 32
    (D) 33

15. Use the tally table. How many glass bottles were recycled in the neighborhood?

    ### Things I See Recycled

Objects	School	Neighborhood
Glass Bottles		ЖЖ
Paper	ЖЖ II	II

    (A) 2
    (B) 5
    (C) 6
    (D) 7

16. The park reused 12 tires to build a playground. The school reused 28 tires to build a playground. How many tires were reused in all?

    (A) 30
    (B) 39
    (C) 40
    (D) 41

© Harcourt

Name _____

Unit B, Review

Choose the best answer. Mark the letter for that answer.

17. It is cool in the forest in the spring. What is the temperature?

    Ⓐ 40°F
    Ⓑ 45°F
    Ⓒ 50°F
    Ⓓ 55°F

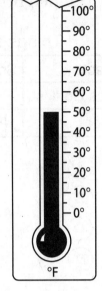

18. There are 3 groups of deer in the forest. Each group has 4 deer. How many deer in all?

    Ⓐ 4
    Ⓑ 6
    Ⓒ 8
    Ⓓ 12

19. Dan recycled 6 bottles on Wednesday. He recycled 5 bottles on Friday. How many bottles did he recycle in all?

    Ⓐ 9
    Ⓑ 10
    Ⓒ 11
    Ⓓ 12

20. Which tool should you use to find out how hot it is in the desert?

    Ⓐ

    Ⓑ

    Ⓒ Ⓓ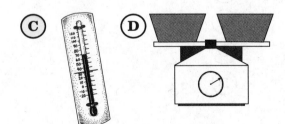

Use with Unit B.

© Harcourt

How Do People Use Rocks and Soil?

Read pages C5 to C7 in your textbook. Then read each question that follows. Decide which is the best answer to each question. Mark the letter for that answer.

1. What is Mount Rushmore?

    Ⓐ a volcano

    Ⓑ a sculpture carved out of a mountain

    Ⓒ the place where four presidents lived

    Ⓓ the name of a town

2. A natural resource comes from —

    Ⓐ the store

    Ⓑ nature

    Ⓒ a lab

    Ⓓ people who make them

3. A brick made of wet clay and straw is —

    Ⓐ boulder

    Ⓑ gravel

    Ⓒ adobe

    Ⓓ rock

4. A hard, nonliving thing that comes from the Earth is —

    Ⓐ soil

    Ⓑ a tree

    Ⓒ a building

    Ⓓ a rock

How Do People Use Plants?

Read pages C9 to C13 in your textbook. Then read each question that follows. Decide which is the best answer to each question. Mark the letter for that answer.

5. What is one way people use plants?

   (A) for making coins

   (B) for making cloth and clothing

   (C) for breaking big rocks

   (D) for blowing bubbles

6. Which one is **NOT** a way plants are used by people?

   (A) to watch television

   (B) as fuel

   (C) for food

   (D) to make medicines

7. What kinds of food come from plants?

   (A) pasta and bread

   (B) spices and oils

   (C) fruits and vegetables

   (D) all of these

8. What happens last when paper is made?

   (A) The pulp is pressed flat to make sheets.

   (B) A tree is cut down.

   (C) Wood chips are made into pulp.

   (D) A pine stool is made.

© Harcourt

How Do People Use Water?

Read pages C15 to C17 in your textbook. Then read each question that follows. Decide which is the best answer to each question. Mark the letter for that answer.

9. What is one way people use water for <u>transportation</u>?

   (A) watering a flower garden
   (B) sailing a boat
   (C) washing their cars
   (D) washing their clothes

10. In this lesson, transportation means —

   (A) ways to move people or things
   (B) the flow of the river
   (C) ways to make electricity
   (D) boats and ships

11. Water makes electricity when the flow of the river —

   (A) moves boats and ships
   (B) is stopped by a dam
   (C) turns machines
   (D) washes clothes

12. People, plants, and animals need water —

   (A) to make electricity
   (B) to wash dishes
   (C) to cook
   (D) to live and grow

© Harcourt

Using Natural Resources

A natural resource is something found in nature that people can use to meet their needs. Rocks, soil, plants, and water are all natural resources.

Choose one of the natural resources listed above. Write a paragraph describing this resource and its uses.

_____

_____

_____

_____

_____

_____

_____

_____

_____

_____

_____

_____

_____

_____

_____

What Is a Fossil?

Read pages C25 to C29 in your textbook. Then read each question that follows. Decide which is the best answer to each question. Mark the letter for that answer.

1. A fish becomes a fossil over many years. First, the fish dies. What is the second thing that happens?

   (A) The print of the fish is left in the rock.

   (B) The fish's body sinks to the ocean floor.

   (C) The fish's body rots.

   (D) The mud turns to rock.

2. What is the name for the hard sap of pine trees?

   (A) a fossil

   (B) amber

   (C) tar

   (D) prints

3. Look at the picture of the mammoth fossil on page C29. What can we tell about the mammoth from looking at its fossil?

   (A) It had long, brown fur.

   (B) It had very good eye sight.

   (C) It had long tusks.

   (D) It ate leaves.

4. A <u>paleontologist</u> is —

   (A) an artist who draws pictures of fossils

   (B) a mechanic who builds electronic dinosaurs

   (C) an artist who makes sculptures of dinosaurs

   (D) a scientist who finds and studies fossils

What Have Scientists Learned from Fossils?

Read pages C31 to C35 in your textbook. Then read each question that follows. Decide which is the best answer to each question. Mark the letter for that answer.

5. Putting a fossil together is a lot like —

   (A) putting together a jigsaw puzzle

   (B) baking a cake

   (C) playing a board game

   (D) taking apart a radio

6. What is the first thing scientists do after they bring a fossil to the museum?

   (A) put it on display

   (B) set all the pieces out on a big table

   (C) glue the pieces together

   (D) clean the pieces

7. How do scientists get fossils out of rock?

   (A) They soak the rock in water until the fossils wash out.

   (B) They carefully chip away at the rock until they free the fossil.

   (C) They break up the rock with hammers.

   (D) They soak the rock in acid.

8. In this lesson, <u>reconstruct</u> means —

   (A) rebuild

   (B) sell

   (C) fix

   (D) paint

What Have Scientists Learned About Dinosaurs?

Read pages C37 to C41 in your textbook. Then read each question that follows. Decide which is the best answer to each question. Mark the letter for that answer.

9. Look at the dinosaur graph on pages C38 and C39. About how tall was a Stegosaurus?

   (A) about 4 feet

   (B) about 10 feet

   (C) about 12 feet

   (D) about 16 feet

10. What does the word <u>dinosaur</u> mean?

    (A) tyrant lizard king

    (B) three-horned face

    (C) fierce ruler

    (D) terrible lizard

11. What will fossils **NOT** tell scientists?

    (A) what dinosaur skin looked like

    (B) what dinosaurs ate

    (C) how tall dinosaurs were

    (D) what color dinosaurs were

12. What did scientists learn when they studied the teeth of Triceratops?

    (A) Triceratops did not have any cavities.

    (B) Triceratops grew a new set of teeth every few years.

    (C) Its teeth were flat like the teeth of today's plant-eating animals.

    (D) Triceratops swallowed its food without chewing it.

© Harcourt

Dinosaurs

A dinosaur is a kind of animal that lived millions of years ago. Scientists have learned about dinosaurs from their fossils.

Suppose you are a paleontologist. You find a scaly fossil print of a dinosaur. In the same area, you also find some flat dinosaur teeth, and a fossil of a dinosaur egg.

Write a paragraph describing what you've found, and what these items tell you about the dinosaur they came from and the surrounding area.

_____

_____

_____

_____

_____

_____

_____

_____

_____

_____

_____

_____

_____

_____

Unit C • Use with Chapter 2.

© Harcourt

Name _____

Unit C, Chapter 1

Choose the best answer. Mark the letter for that answer.

1. Which rock has a mass greater than the mass of the box of crayons?

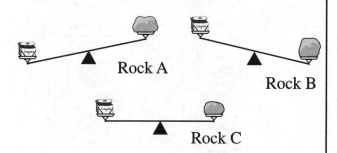

Rock A

Rock B

Rock C

Ⓐ   Rock A

Ⓑ   Rock B

Ⓒ   Rock C

2. About how long is the rock?

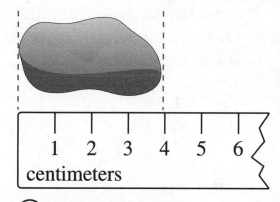

Ⓐ   1 centimeter

Ⓑ   2 centimeters

Ⓒ   3 centimeters

Ⓓ   4 centimeters

3. What is the temperature?

Ⓐ   40°F

Ⓑ   45°F

Ⓒ   50°F

Ⓓ   55°F

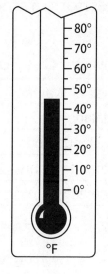

4. Ann started to make a bird feeder at

She finished 15 minutes later. What time did she finish?

Ⓐ   4:15

Ⓑ   4:30

Ⓒ   4:45

Ⓓ   5:00

Go On

© Harcourt

Math Practice

Unit C, Chapter 1

Choose the best answer. Mark the letter for that answer.

Use the tally table to answer Questions 5 and 6.

How Our Class Uses Water in One Day

Uses of Water	How Many Times
Drinking	ЖЖ ЖЖ |||
Washing hands	ЖЖ ЖЖ	
Watering plants	|||
Cleaning	ЖЖ

5. How many more times did the class use water for washing hands than for cleaning?

   (A) 3
   (B) 4
   (C) 5
   (D) 6

6. Which way did the class use water **MOST**?

   (A) cleaning
   (B) washing hands
   (C) drinking
   (D) watering plants

7. Are you more likely to pull a picture of an apple or grapes from the bag?

   (A) apple
   (B) grapes

8. It takes 2 cups of water to brush your teeth. There are five people in the family. How many cups of water does the family use in all?

   (A) 4
   (B) 6
   (C) 8
   (D) 10

© Harcourt

Name _____

Math Practice

Unit C, Chapter 2

Choose the best answer. Mark the letter for that answer.

9. Jared has 13 plant fossils and 6 animal fossils. How many fossils does Jared have in all?

   (A) 9
   (B) 19
   (C) 21
   (D) 29

11. How long is this fossil?

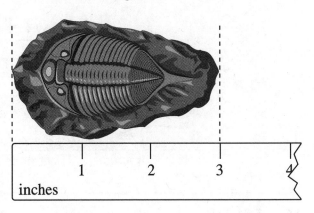

   (A) 2 inches
   (B) 3 inches
   (C) 4 inches
   (D) 5 inches

10. About how many rocks are in the jar?

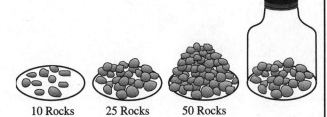

10 Rocks   25 Rocks   50 Rocks

   (A) about 5
   (B) about 10
   (C) about 25
   (D) about 50

12. How much longer was the Stegosaurus than Scelidosaurus?

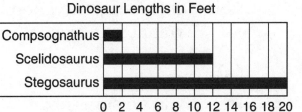

Dinosaur Lengths in Feet

   (A) 4 feet   (C) 8 feet
   (B) 6 feet   (D) 10 feet

© Harcourt

Go On

Name _____

Unit C, Chapter 2

Choose the best answer. Mark the letter for that answer.

Use the graph to answer Questions 13 and 14.

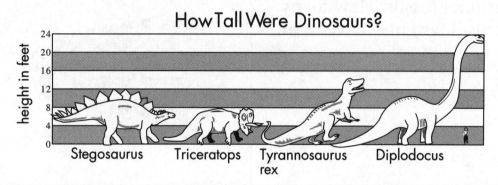

How Tall Were Dinosaurs?

13. Which dinosaur was the tallest?
   Ⓐ Stegosaurus
   Ⓑ Triceratops
   Ⓒ Tyrannosaurus rex
   Ⓓ Diplodocus

14. Which list shows the dinosaurs in order from shortest to tallest?
   Ⓐ Diplodocus, Triceratops, Tyrannosaurus rex, Stegosaurus
   Ⓑ Triceratops, Tyrannosaurus rex, Stegosaurus, Diplodocus
   Ⓒ Triceratops, Stegosaurus, Tyrannosaurus rex, Diplodocus
   Ⓓ Stegosaurus, Diplodocus, Tyrannosaurus rex, Triceratops

15. Which object is less than 1 foot long?
   Ⓐ baseball bat
   Ⓑ car
   Ⓒ key
   Ⓓ bicycle

16. Choose the reasonable answer. A scientist found 32 dinosaur fossils in Colorado and 27 dinosaur fossils in Montana. How many fossils did she find in all?
   Ⓐ 55
   Ⓑ 59
   Ⓒ 68
   Ⓓ 69

© Harcourt

Math Practice

Unit C, Review

Choose the best answer. Mark the letter for that answer.

17. Which tool should you use to measure how long a fossil is?

(A)

(B)

(C)

(D)

18. The paleontologist found 5 fossils in tar, 8 fossils in rock, and 3 fossils in amber. How many fossils did the paleontologist find in all?

(A) 13

(B) 14

(C) 15

(D) 16

19. Paul has 4 marble rocks and 8 lava rocks. Which number sentence shows how many rocks he has in all?

(A) $4 + 4 = 8$

(B) $8 + 8 = 16$

(C) $4 + 8 = 12$

(D) $8 - 4 = 4$

20. Scelidosaurus was about 12 feet long. Compsognathus was about 2 feet long. About how much longer was Scelidosaurus than Compsognathus?

(A) about 1 foot

(B) about 10 feet

(C) about 11 feet

(D) about 14 feet

What Are Stars and Planets?

Read pages D5 to D11 in your textbook. Then read each question that follows. Decide which is the best answer to each question. Mark the letter for that answer.

1. On a clear night, you can see —
   - (A) one or two bright stars
   - (B) a few stars
   - (C) many stars
   - (D) all the stars

2. A constellation in this lesson means —
   - (A) a group of stars that are very close together
   - (B) a group of stars that form a picture
   - (C) a place where scientists study stars
   - (D) a tool for looking at the stars

3. Look at the picture of the Milky Way on pages D6–D7. What is the Milky Way?
   - (A) a very large group of stars
   - (B) a constellation that looks like a milk bottle
   - (C) the path Earth takes around the sun
   - (D) a patch of sky where there aren't any stars

4. What does a telescope do?
   - (A) It makes things look farther away.
   - (B) It makes things look smaller.
   - (C) It makes bright things look dull so you can look at them more easily.
   - (D) It makes things look closer and larger.

© Harcourt

What Causes Day and Night?

Read pages D13 to D17 in your textbook. Then read each question that follows. Decide which is the best answer to each question. Mark the letter for that answer.

5. What causes day and night?

Ⓐ The sun is crossing the sky.

Ⓑ The moon is circling Earth.

Ⓒ Earth is rotating.

Ⓓ The sky is moving.

6. In this lesson, solar energy means —

Ⓐ the star closest to Earth

Ⓑ daytime

Ⓒ nighttime

Ⓓ light or heat from the sun

7. The sun shines on —

Ⓐ the whole Earth at the same time

Ⓑ the side of Earth that is facing the sun

Ⓒ the top half of Earth only

Ⓓ the southern part of Earth only

8. How many times does Earth rotate in one day?

Ⓐ once

Ⓑ twice

Ⓒ twelve times

Ⓓ twenty-four times

© Harcourt

What Causes the Seasons?

Read pages D19 to D23 in your textbook. Then read each question that follows. Decide which is the best answer to each question. Mark the letter for that answer.

9. Which of these never changes?

Ⓐ the side of Earth that faces the sun

Ⓑ where Earth is in its orbit

Ⓒ the tilt of Earth's axis

Ⓓ the seasons

10. Which of these is **NOT** a season?

Ⓐ spring

Ⓑ summer

Ⓒ orbit

Ⓓ winter

11. Which word means the same as the underlined word?

Earth is always <u>tilted</u> in the same direction.

Ⓐ rotating

Ⓑ slanted

Ⓒ shaded

Ⓓ turned

12. We have seasons because —

Ⓐ the sun shines on the moon

Ⓑ Earth is tilted and it moves around the sun

Ⓒ Earth turns on its axis

Ⓓ Earth has clouds

How Does the Moon Move and Change?

Read pages D25 to D29 in your textbook. Then read each question that follows. Decide which is the best answer to each question. Mark the letter for that answer.

13. Why does the moon seem to shine?

(A) It is a hot ball of burning gases.

(B) Light from Earth shines on the moon and makes it look bright.

(C) The sun shines on the moon and makes it look bright.

(D) Craters make the moon look bright.

14. Ella made this calendar. When will she see the next full moon?

May

Sunday	Monday	Tuesday	Wednesday	Thursday	Friday	Saturday
1 full moon	2	3	4	5	6	7 quarter moon
8	9	10	11	12	13	14 new moon
15	16	17	18	19	20	21 quarter moon
22	23	24	25	26	27	28
29	30	31				

(A) May 22

(B) May 24

(C) May 28

(D) June 7

15. Mickey, Frank, Mary Rose, and Keisha drew these pictures of Earth, the moon, and the sun. Whose picture shows something that can never happen?

(A) Mickey's art:

Earth Sun Moon

(B) Frank's art:

Earth Moon Sun

(C) Mary Rose's art:

Moon Earth Sun

(D) Keisha's art:

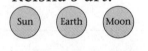
Sun Earth Moon

16. What is the **MOST** important idea of the paragraphs on page D28?

(A) The moon takes four weeks to orbit Earth.

(B) We cannot see the new moon from Earth.

(C) The sun shines on the part of the moon that faces it.

(D) The moon's orbit makes the moon seem to change shape.

Day and Night

Day and night are caused by Earth's rotation. Earth spins round and round in space. This spinning is called rotation.

Write a paragraph describing how Earth's rotation causes day and night.

_____

_____

_____

_____

_____

_____

_____

_____

_____

_____

_____

_____

_____

_____

© Harcourt

How Does Weather Change?

Read pages D37 to D41 in your textbook. Then read each question that follows. Decide which is the best answer to each question. Mark the letter for that answer.

1. In this lesson, <u>weather</u> means —

   Ⓐ changes in the seasons

   Ⓑ what the air is like outside

   Ⓒ the temperature inside

   Ⓓ thunderstorms

2. Warmer, wetter spring weather —

   Ⓐ helps plants grow new leaves and flowers

   Ⓑ makes weather change quickly

   Ⓒ makes leaves drop off trees

   Ⓓ makes plants die

3. Which of these is a FACT about winter?

   Ⓐ In all places, there is snow in winter.

   Ⓑ Winter is the warmest time of the year.

   Ⓒ Winter is the coldest time of the year.

   Ⓓ In winter leaves begin to fall off the trees.

4. What is the weather often like in the summer?

   Ⓐ warm and wet

   Ⓑ cool and sometimes cloudy

   Ⓒ very cold

   Ⓓ sunny and hot

Name _____

What Is the Water Cycle?

Read pages D43 to D45 in your textbook. Then read each question that follows. Decide which is the best answer to each question. Mark the letter for that answer.

5. What happens to water when it evaporates?

   (A) It turns to ice.

   (B) It becomes snow.

   (C) It changes into a gas.

   (D) It changes into tiny drops of water.

6. Which happens after water vapor meets cool air?

   (A) Drops of water form a cloud.

   (B) Heat from the sun makes ocean water evaporate.

   (C) Water vapor changes into drops of water.

   (D) Water drops become heavy and fall as rain.

7. What must happen so it can rain?

   (A) Water drops in the air must become heavy.

   (B) Water drops in the air have to evaporate.

   (C) It has to be cold on the ground.

   (D) Water drops in the air must form icy flakes.

8. Look at the picture on pages D44 and D45. Which way does the water flow?

   (A) from the mountain to the stream to the ocean

   (B) from the stream to the mountain to the ocean

   (C) from the ocean to the stream to the mountain

   (D) from the ocean to the mountain to the stream

© Harcourt

How Do We Measure Weather Conditions?

Read pages D47 to D51 in your textbook. Then read each question that follows. Decide which is the best answer to each question. Mark the letter for that answer.

9. An <u>anemometer</u> measures —

　Ⓐ　how fast the wind is blowing

　Ⓑ　which way the wind is blowing

　Ⓒ　how much rain has fallen

　Ⓓ　the temperature

10. Which of these is **NOT** a tool meteorologists use to measure weather conditions?

　Ⓐ　anemometer

　Ⓑ　rain gauge

　Ⓒ　wind vane

　Ⓓ　temperature

11. How might the weather change when you see stratus clouds?

　Ⓐ　It may turn sunny.

　Ⓑ　A thunderstorm may form.

　Ⓒ　It may rain or snow.

　Ⓓ　It may be fair weather.

12. What does the lesson say cumulus clouds look like?

　Ⓐ　feathers

　Ⓑ　streaks

　Ⓒ　smoke

　Ⓓ　puffy cotton

© Harcourt

How Can We Prepare For Weather?

Read pages D53 to D57 in your textbook. Then read each question that follows. Decide which is the best answer to each question. Mark the letter for that answer.

13. Which of the following storms involves snow?

Ⓐ hurricane
Ⓑ blizzard
Ⓒ thunderstorm
Ⓓ tornado

14. Which of the following is **NOT** something you should do to protect yourself on a sunny day?

Ⓐ use sunscreen
Ⓑ wear a hat with a brim
Ⓒ wear sunglasses
Ⓓ wear rain boots

15. A hurricane has —

Ⓐ strong winds
Ⓑ high ocean waves
Ⓒ heavy rain
Ⓓ all of these

16. In a thunderstorm, you should —

Ⓐ cover windows with plywood
Ⓑ wear layers of clothing
Ⓒ go stand near a tree
Ⓓ stay away from water

© Harcourt

Storms

Storms can be very dangerous. Some types of storms include hurricanes, tornados, blizzards, and thunderstorms.

Pick one of the storms listed above. Do research to find out what causes that kind of storm. Write about the storm you chose. Describe what happens to cause it and what the storm is like.

_____

_____

_____

_____

_____

_____

_____

_____

_____

_____

_____

Unit D, Chapter 1

Choose the best answer. Mark the letter for that answer.

Use the calendar to answer
Questions 1 and 2.

May

Sunday	Monday	Tuesday	Wednesday	Thursday	Friday	Saturday
						1
2	3	4	5	6	7	8
9	10	11	12	13	14	15
16	17	18	19	20	21	22
23	24	25	26	27	28	29
30	31					

1. What is the date of the first Friday in May?

   (A) May 1
   (B) May 2
   (C) May 5
   (D) May 7

2. On this calendar Memorial Day is on the last day of May. On which day of the week is Memorial Day?

   (A) Sunday
   (B) Monday
   (C) Friday
   (D) Saturday

Use the calendar to answer
Questions 3 and 4.

March

Sunday	Monday	Tuesday	Wednesday	Thursday	Friday	Saturday
		1	2	3	4	5
6	7	8	9	10	11	12
13	14	15	16	17	18	19
20	21	22	23	24	25	26
27	28	29	30	31		

3. Spring begins on March 21. On which day of the week does spring begin?

   (A) Sunday
   (B) Monday
   (C) Tuesday
   (D) Thursday

4. The class field trip is on the third Thursday in March. What is the date of the trip?

   (A) March 3
   (B) March 10
   (C) March 17
   (D) March 24

© Harcourt

Unit D, Chapter 1

Choose the best answer. Mark the letter for that answer.

5. The Big Dipper and the Little Dipper each have 7 stars. How many stars do they have in all?

  Ⓐ 11

  Ⓑ 12

  Ⓒ 13

  Ⓓ 14

6. The clock shows the time the sun will rise tomorrow.

At what time can you see the sunrise tomorrow?

  Ⓐ 6:20

  Ⓑ 6:30

  Ⓒ 6:35

  Ⓓ 6:40

7. Jack left school at

He arrived home 30 minutes later. At what time did Jack arrive home?

  Ⓐ 3:00

  Ⓑ 3:30

  Ⓒ 12:00

  Ⓓ 12:30

8. Mary saw about 35 birds in the sky in the morning. She saw about 45 birds in the sky in the afternoon. About how many birds did she see in all?

  Ⓐ 70

  Ⓑ 80

  Ⓒ 85

  Ⓓ 90

© Harcourt

Name _____

Unit D, Chapter 2

Math Practice

Choose the best answer. Mark the letter for that answer.

9. Use the graph to answer the question. Which season is the favorite of nine children?

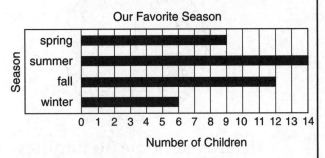

Our Favorite Season

Number of Children

Ⓐ spring   Ⓒ fall

Ⓑ summer   Ⓓ winter

10. To make a rain gauge which tool should you use to measure the number of inches of rainfall?

Ⓐ

Ⓑ

Ⓒ

Ⓓ

Use the tally table to answer Questions 11 and 12.

Weather in July

Type of Weather	Tally Marks
sunny	卌 II
cloudy	卌 IIII
rainy	卌 卌

11. Which kind of day happened **MOST** in July?

Ⓐ cloudy

Ⓑ rainy

Ⓒ sunny

12. Which kind of day happened **LEAST** in July?

Ⓐ cloudy

Ⓑ sunny

Ⓒ rainy

Go On

Name _____

Unit D, Chapter 2

Choose the best answer. Mark the letter for that answer.

13. Which thermometer shows a temperature of 80°F?

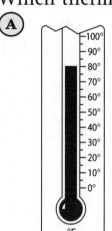 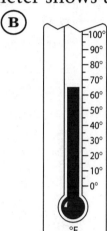 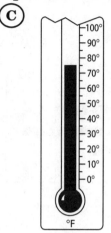 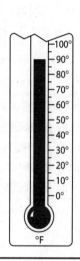

Use the chart to answer Questions 14 and 15.

Weather Conditions

Day	Weather
Sunday	cloudy
Monday	cloudy
Tuesday	cloudy and rainy
Wednesday	cloudy and rainy
Thursday	sunny with clouds
Friday	sunny and clear
Saturday	sunny and clear

14. How many days were cloudy and rainy?

- (A) 1
- (B) 2
- (C) 3
- (D) 4

15. Which days were sunny and clear?

- (A) Wednesday and Thursday
- (B) Friday and Saturday
- (C) Thursday and Saturday
- (D) Monday and Friday

16. Pat collected the rain water that fell on Friday. How much rain fell on Friday?

- (A) 0 inches
- (B) 1 inch
- (C) 2 inches
- (D) 3 inches

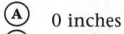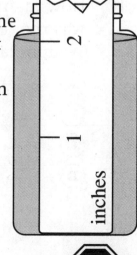

Unit D, Review

Choose the best answer. Mark the letter for that answer.

Use the graph to answer
Questions 17 and 18.

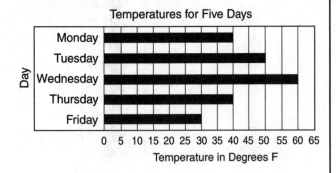

Temperatures for Five Days

19. Jack counted 12 bright stars
in the sky on Sunday night.
Peg counted 19 bright stars
in the sky Sunday night.
How many more bright stars
did Peg count than Jack?

    (A) 7

    (B) 8

    (C) 21

    (D) 31

17. Which day had the highest
temperature?

    (A) Monday

    (B) Tuesday

    (C) Wednesday

    (D) Friday

20. Which tool is used to measure
how many inches of snow
have fallen?

    (A)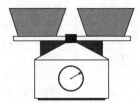

18. How many degrees warmer
was the temperature on
Wednesday than Thursday?

    (A) 10°F

    (B) 15°F

    (C) 20°F

    (D) 25°F

    (B)

    (C)    (D)

© Harcourt

What Is Matter?

Read pages E5 to E7 in your textbook. Then read each question that follows. Decide which is the best answer to each question. Mark the letter for that answer.

1. In this lesson, <u>matter</u> is —

   (A) what all things are made of

   (B) the space something takes up

   (C) the mass of something

   (D) the color, size, and shape of things

2. What is the **MOST** important idea of the paragraph on page E6?

   (A) A chair is a solid.

   (B) Matter has three forms: solid, liquid, and gas.

   (C) Matter has certain properties.

   (D) The air in a balloon is a gas.

3. The juice on page E6 is an example of a —

   (A) solid

   (B) gas

   (C) solid and gas

   (D) liquid

4. Which sentence tells a property of the chair on page E6?

   (A) No one is sitting on it.

   (B) It is on the floor.

   (C) It is orange.

   (D) It is from the kindergarten room.

© Harcourt

What Can We Find Out About Solids?

Read pages E9 to E13 in your textbook. Then read each question that follows. Decide which is the best answer to each question. Mark the letter for that answer.

5. Look at the chart on page E13. The box is —

   (A) longer than the wood

   (B) shorter than the wood

   (C) heavier than the wood

   (D) the same size as the wood

6. What property of the crayons on page E11 makes them different from one another?

   (A) length

   (B) shape

   (C) use

   (D) color

7. Ben grouped some of the objects on pages E10 and E11. Here is the chart he made. Which object does not belong?

   Things that have bumps on them

   (A) twig

   (B) dinosaur

   (C) baseball

   (D) paper clip

8. A <u>centimeter</u> is a unit used to measure —

   (A) weight

   (B) length

   (C) mass

   (D) size

© Harcourt

What Can We Find Out About Liquids?

Read pages E15 to E19 in your textbook. Then read each question that follows. Decide which is the best answer to each question. Mark the letter for that answer.

9. Which is **NOT** true?
   - (A) Liquids have mass.
   - (B) Liquids have volume.
   - (C) Liquids do not change in amount unless you add more or take some away.
   - (D) Liquids have shape.

10. If you pour juice into a bottle, it will —
   - (A) change in amount
   - (B) take the shape of the bottle
   - (C) keep its shape
   - (D) take up less space

11. Look at this measuring cup. Which arrow points to 125 milliliters?

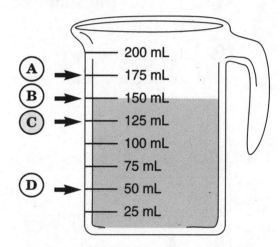

12. A <u>milliliter</u> is a unit used to measure —
   - (A) weight
   - (B) height
   - (C) volume
   - (D) mass

© Harcourt

What Can We Find Out About Gases?

Read pages E21 to E25 in your textbook. Then read each question that follows. Decide which is the best answer to each question. Mark the letter for that answer.

13. How is a gas like a liquid?

   Ⓐ It has no mass.

   Ⓑ You can see through it.

   Ⓒ It takes the shape of its container.

   Ⓓ It fills all the space inside a container.

14. What did Garrett Morgan invent?

   Ⓐ the hot-air balloon

   Ⓑ the gas mask

   Ⓒ the air pump

   Ⓓ the gas grill

15. Look at the rod the girl is holding on pages E24 and E25. Suppose you took off the balloon filled with air and taped the yellow balloon in its place. What would happen?

   Ⓐ The rod would tilt the same way it is tilting now.

   Ⓑ The rod would tilt the other way.

   Ⓒ The balloon would begin to rise.

   Ⓓ The rod would begin to turn.

16. Which of these is an OPINION about air?

   Ⓐ It fills the space of its container.

   Ⓑ It is made up of gases.

   Ⓒ It can lift a kite.

   Ⓓ It feels good when it blows on me.

© Harcourt

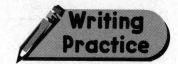

Forms of Matter

Matter has three forms—solid, liquid, and gas. Each form has its own specific characteristics.

Write a paragraph in which you compare and contrast the characteristics of the different forms of matter.

_____

_____

_____

_____

_____

_____

_____

_____

_____

_____

_____

_____

_____

_____

© Harcourt

What Happens When You Mix Matter?

Read pages E33 to E37 in your textbook. Then read each question that follows. Decide which is the best answer to each question. Mark the letter for that answer.

1. How could you change the mass of the loaf of bread on page E34?

    (A) Cut each slice in half.

    (B) Cut the rest of the bread into slices.

    (C) Arrange the slices so they form a different shape.

    (D) Eat a slice.

2. Which of these is a mixture?

    (A) peas

    (B) carrots

    (C) corn

    (D) rice and beans

3. Which is **NOT** an example of solid matter?

    (A) an orange

    (B) an orange crayon

    (C) orange juice

    (D) an orange tree

4. Which of these is **NOT** a FACT from the lesson?

    (A) Cutting is one way to change matter.

    (B) Changing the shape of matter changes its mass.

    (C) A mixture is made up of two or more things.

    (D) Matter can be cut and mixed.

© Harcourt

How Can Water Change?

Read pages E39 to E43 in your textbook. Then read each question that follows. Decide which is the best answer to each question. Mark the letter for that answer.

5. Water as a solid may be —
    (A) ice
    (B) water vapor
    (C) a puddle
    (D) rain

6. What happens after water boils?
    (A) It turns into a solid.
    (B) It melts.
    (C) It begins to evaporate.
    (D) It condenses.

7. If the temperature goes above 0°C, ice —
    (A) boils
    (B) melts
    (C) evaporates
    (D) condenses

8. <u>Reversible</u> in this lesson means —
    (A) not able to change back to the way it was
    (B) not able to change from solid to liquid
    (C) able to change back to the way it was
    (D) not able to change from vapor to liquid

© Harcourt

What Other Ways Does Matter Change?

Read pages E45 to E49 in your textbook. Then read each question that follows. Decide which is the best answer to each question. Mark the letter for that answer.

9. Which step in making gelatin happens last?

   Ⓐ The hot liquid mixture begins to cool.

   Ⓑ The gelatin powder is mixed with hot water.

   Ⓒ The gelatin becomes firm.

   Ⓓ The solid gelatin powder is put into a bowl.

10. Which change is reversible?

    Ⓐ toasting a marshmallow

    Ⓑ cooking a hamburger

    Ⓒ mashing potatoes

    Ⓓ mixing raisins in your cereal

11. Which change is irreversible?

    Ⓐ scrambling an egg

    Ⓑ folding a sheet of paper

    Ⓒ turning on a light

    Ⓓ bending a stick into the shape of a heart

12. An uncooked egg is one that is not cooked. What does the word part un- mean?

    Ⓐ hot

    Ⓑ mixed

    Ⓒ not

    Ⓓ hard

© Harcourt

Water Changes

Water can exist as a solid, a liquid, or a gas. Freezing, condensing, evaporating, and melting are the ways water moves between its different forms.

Describe each of the processes listed above.

_____

_____

_____

_____

_____

_____

_____

_____

_____

_____

_____

_____

_____

_____

_____

© Harcourt

Unit E, Chapter 1

Choose the best answer. Mark the letter for that answer.

1. Which unit is used to measure length?

   (A) milliliter

   (B) centimeter

   (C) cup

   (D) degree

2. Which unit is used to measure the volume of a liquid?

   (A) degree

   (B) centimeter

   (C) inch

   (D) milliliter

Use the picture below to answer Questions 3 and 4.

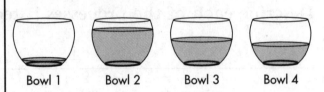

Bowl 1   Bowl 2   Bowl 3   Bowl 4

3. Which bowl is holding the least mass?

   (A) Bowl 1

   (B) Bowl 2

   (C) Bowl 3

   (D) Bowl 4

4. Which answer shows the bowls listed in order from greatest mass to least mass?

   (A) Bowl 1, Bowl 2, Bowl 3, Bowl 4

   (B) Bowl 2, Bowl 3, Bowl 4, Bowl 1

   (C) Bowl 2, Bowl 3, Bowl 1, Bowl 4

   (D) Bowl 1, Bowl 3, Bowl 2, Bowl 4

© Harcourt

Unit E, Chapter 1

Choose the best answer. Mark the letter for that answer.

5. Which list shows the animals in order from least mass to greatest mass?

- Ⓐ bird, raccoon, elephant
- Ⓑ elephant, raccoon, bird
- Ⓒ raccoon, bird, elephant
- Ⓓ bird, elephant, raccoon

6. About how long is this piece of chalk?

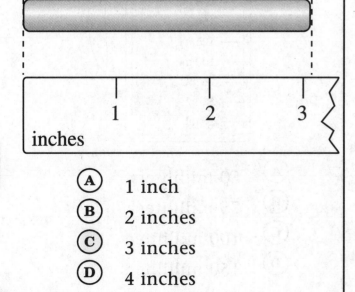

- Ⓐ 1 inch
- Ⓑ 2 inches
- Ⓒ 3 inches
- Ⓓ 4 inches

7. About how long is this nail?

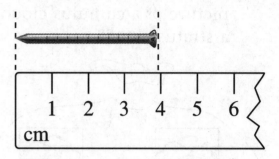

- Ⓐ 1 centimeter
- Ⓑ 2 centimeters
- Ⓒ 3 centimeters
- Ⓓ 4 centimeters

8. Which tool should you use to measure the volume of water in a glass?

Ⓐ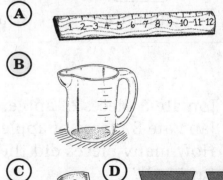

Ⓑ

Ⓒ   Ⓓ

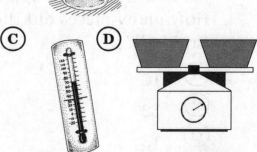

Stop

© Harcourt

Math
Practice

Unit E, Chapter 2

Choose the best answer. Mark the letter for that answer.

9. Are you more likely to pull a picture of a cumulus cloud or a stratus cloud?

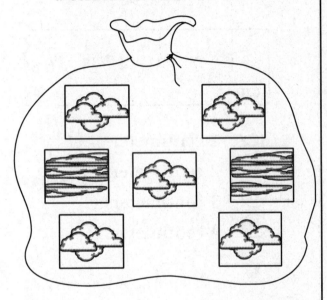

 (A)

cumulus

(B)

stratus

10. Jon ate 5 pieces of apple. Jane ate 8 pieces of apple. How many pieces did they eat in all?

(A) 10

(B) 12

(C) 13

(D) 14

11. An apple slice had a mass of 4. After the slice dried, the slice had a mass of 2. Which number sentence shows how much mass the apple slice lost?

(A) $2 + 2 = 4$

(B) $4 + 2 = 6$

(C) $6 - 4 = 2$

(D) $4 - 2 = 2$

12. How much water is in the measuring cup?

200 mL
175 mL
150 mL
125 mL
100 mL
75 mL
50 mL
25 mL

(A) 50 milliliters

(B) 75 milliliters

(C) 100 milliliters

(D) 150 milliliters

© Harcourt

Go On

Unit E, Chapter 2

Choose the best answer. Mark the letter for that answer.

13. Karen placed a measuring cup with 75 milliliters of water on a windowsill in the sun. Three days later, the measuring cup held only 65 milliliters of water. Which number sentence shows how many milliliters of the water evaporated, or changed to a gas?

   (A) $75 - 65 = 10$

   (B) $65 - 10 = 55$

   (C) $75 + 10 = 85$

   (D) $75 + 65 = 140$

14. Dan put 8 paper clips, 5 tacks, and 6 rubber bands on one side of a balance. How many objects did he put on that side of the balance?

   (A) 17

   (B) 18

   (C) 19

   (D) 20

15. Ann counted 56 almonds and 37 peanuts in her snack mixture. How many nuts were there in all?

    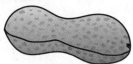

   (A) 93

   (B) 193

   (C) 390

   (D) 930

16. Which tool should you use to find out if a balloon full of air has a greater mass than a balloon with no air?

   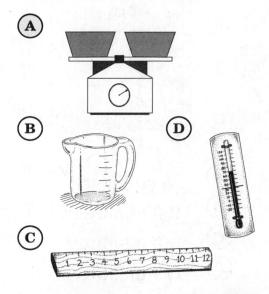

Unit E, Review

Choose the best answer. Mark the letter for that answer.

17. About how long is the pen?

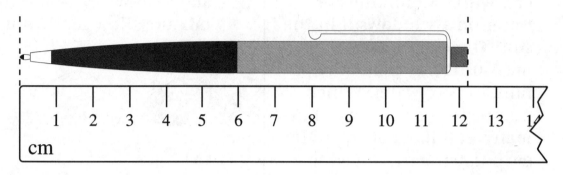

(A) 11 centimeters

(B) 12 centimeters

(C) 13 centimeters

(D) 14 centimeters

---

18. How much water is in the measuring cup?

(A) 75 milliliters

(B) 100 milliliters

(C) 150 milliliters

(D) 175 milliliters

19. Sandy put 5 tomato slices, 6 carrot slices, and 3 cucumber slices in her salad. How many slices did she put in her salad in all?

(A) 9

(B) 11

(C) 12

(D) 14

20. Which unit should you use to measure the length of a stick?

(A) centimeter

(B) milliliter

(C) degree

(D) cup

What Are Forces?

Read pages F5 to F11 in your textbook. Then read each question that follows. Decide which is the best answer to each question. Mark the letter for that answer.

1. Which tells you something's location?

   Ⓐ under the couch

   Ⓑ running around

   Ⓒ speaking softly

   Ⓓ in a little while

2. The force that pulls things toward the center of Earth is called —

   Ⓐ wind

   Ⓑ magnetism

   Ⓒ gravity

   Ⓓ electricity

3. Wind is —

   Ⓐ clouds

   Ⓑ moving air

   Ⓒ warm air

   Ⓓ cold weather

4. Which of these is **NOT** an example of a force?

   Ⓐ magnetism

   Ⓑ moving water

   Ⓒ direction

   Ⓓ pushing a ball

How Do Magnets Work?

Read pages F13 to F17 in your textbook. Then read each question that follows. Decide which is the best answer to each question. Mark the letter for that answer.

5. A piece of iron or steel that attracts other objects made of iron and steel is a —

   (A) pole

   (B) compass

   (C) magnet

   (D) needle

6. A magnet is **NOT** used in making which of the following?

   (A) telephones

   (B) books

   (C) computers

   (D) doorbells

7. Opposite magnetic poles _____ one another.

   (A) attract

   (B) have no effect on

   (C) repel

   (D) unbalance

8. On a compass, the needle always points to the —

   (A) north

   (B) south

   (C) east

   (D) west

© Harcourt

How Can We Measure Motion?

Read pages F19 to F23 in your textbook. Then read each question that follows. Decide which is the best answer to each question. Mark the letter for that answer.

9. Which of these is a FACT from the lesson?

   (A) It takes less force to move something heavy than something light.

   (B) It takes more force to move something a long distance than a short distance.

   (C) It takes less force to move something over a rough surface than over a smooth surface.

   (D) It takes more force to move something little than big.

10. When something is in motion, it —

    (A) is moving

    (B) stays still

    (C) is a force

    (D) is going a long way

11. Daria wants to do the experiment shown on page F23. She made a list of the things she will need, but she left something out. What was it?

Things Used to Measure Force	
1. cardboard	4. paper clip
2. stapler	5. rubber band
3. book	6. string

    (A) a tape measure

    (B) staples

    (C) tape

    (D) a marker

12. Which of these is NOT a measure of motion?

    (A) how far something goes

    (B) how much time something takes to go from one spot to another

    (C) how much force it takes to pull something

    (D) how much friction there is

© Harcourt

Forces

A push or pull that makes something move is called a force. Wind and gravity are both kinds of forces.

Choose one of the forces mentioned above. Write a paragraph describing this force.

_____

_____

_____

_____

_____

_____

_____

_____

_____

_____

_____

_____

_____

© Harcourt

What Is Sound?

Read pages F31 to F35 in your textbook. Then read each question that follows. Decide which is the best answer to each question. Mark the letter for that answer.

1. What is an <u>audiologist</u>?

    Ⓐ a teacher

    Ⓑ someone who tests people's hearing

    Ⓒ someone who tests sound equipment

    Ⓓ a heart doctor

2. You make sounds using your —

    Ⓐ eyes

    Ⓑ ears

    Ⓒ ribs

    Ⓓ vocal cords

3. How are your eardrums and vocal cords alike?

    Ⓐ They have the same shape.

    Ⓑ They are both in your throat.

    Ⓒ They both vibrate.

    Ⓓ They both help you make sounds.

4. In this lesson, <u>vibrate</u> means —

    Ⓐ let you hear

    Ⓑ move in every direction

    Ⓒ move back and forth

    Ⓓ move slowly

© Harcourt

How Do Sounds Vary?

Read pages F37 to F39 in your textbook. Then read each question that follows. Decide which is the best answer to each question. Mark the letter for that answer.

5. Which of these is a FACT from the lesson?

  (A) Sounds are all the same.

  (B) It takes more energy to make a high sound than a low sound.

  (C) Sounds are all around you.

  (D) You can see all sounds.

6. Which of these is **NOT** a FACT from the lesson?

  (A) It takes more energy to make a soft sound than a loud sound.

  (B) Sounds are different in loudness.

  (C) Sounds are different in pitch.

  (D) A bullfrog's croak is an example of a low-pitched sound.

7. In this lesson, <u>pitch</u> means —

  (A) how loud or soft a sound is

  (B) how high or low a sound is

  (C) how much energy a sound has

  (D) how different sounds are heard

8. Which of these is an example of a loud sound?

  (A) a person whispering

  (B) a bee buzzing

  (C) a person turning the pages of a book

  (D) a person shouting

© Harcourt

How Does Sound Travel?

Read pages F41 to F45 in your textbook. Then read each question that follows. Decide which is the best answer to each question. Mark the letter for that answer.

9. What is the **MOST** important idea of the two paragraphs on page F43?

   Ⓐ The air makes the cup vibrate.

   Ⓑ The cup makes the string vibrate.

   Ⓒ Sounds can travel through solid objects.

   Ⓓ A person talks into one cup, making the air inside vibrate.

10. Sounds can travel through —

    Ⓐ only gases and solids

    Ⓑ only gases and liquids

    Ⓒ only gases

    Ⓓ gases, solids, and liquids

11. Sonar in this lesson means —

    Ⓐ a way to find things that are lost

    Ⓑ a way to use sounds to locate things under water

    Ⓒ a way to use sounds to locate things in space

    Ⓓ the way whales talk to each other

12. Which of these is an example of sound traveling through solids?

    Ⓐ a person hearing a bell ring

    Ⓑ people talking through a string telephone

    Ⓒ dolphins locating objects

    Ⓓ whales communicating

How Can We Make Different Sounds?

Read pages F47 to F49 in your textbook. Then read each question that follows. Decide which is the best answer to each question. Mark the letter for that answer.

13. The faster a string vibrates, the —

(A) higher the sound

(B) lower the sound

(C) longer the sound

(D) shorter the sound

14. Look at the picture on page F48. How is the boy's cup like a musical instrument?

(A) They have the same shape.

(B) They are both made of metal.

(C) You can produce sound by blowing into them.

(D) They both have strings.

15. This lesson tells you about all of the following EXCEPT —

(A) how to give a stringed instrument a higher sound

(B) how to make a drum sound softer

(C) the difference in sound between thin strings and thick strings

(D) how dolphins communicate

16. Which of these is NOT a FACT from the lesson?

(A) You cannot change the loudness of a sound.

(B) Hitting a drum with a lot of energy makes a loud sound.

(C) Tapping a drum lightly makes a soft sound.

(D) Some musical instruments have strings.

© Harcourt

Writing Practice

Sound

Sound is the energy that lets you hear. Sounds are often different in their loudness and pitch.

Write a paragraph about loudness and pitch. Explain what they are and how they can make sounds different. Give examples.

_____

_____

_____

_____

_____

_____

_____

_____

_____

_____

_____

_____

_____

© Harcourt

Name_____

Unit F, Chapter 1

Choose the best answer. Mark the letter for that answer.

1. Susan and Laura each pushed a ball. Susan's ball went 54 inches. Laura's ball went 18 inches. How much farther did Susan's ball go than Laura's?

   (A) 36 inches

   (B) 44 inches

   (C) 46 inches

   (D) 72 inches

2. Which tool should you use to measure how long it takes to run a race?

   (A) rubber band

   (B) meterstick

   (C) stopwatch

   (D) thermometer

3. Pat used a force of 200. Sally used a force of 75. Who used the greatest force?

   (A) Sally

   (B) Pat

4. The scale in the pictures below measures the amount of force used by each person.

   Picture A

   Picture B

   Which picture shows the greater force?

   (A) Picture A

   (B) Picture B

Go On

Math Practice

Unit F, Chapter 1

Choose the best answer. Mark the letter for that answer.

Use the data in the table to answer Question 5.

Person	Amount of Force
Sam	185
Jan	75

5. How much more force did Sam use than Jan?

   Ⓐ 100

   Ⓑ 110

   Ⓒ 250

   Ⓓ 260

6. Carol finished the race in 41 seconds. Kim finished the race in 38 seconds. Who ran faster?

   Ⓐ Carol

   Ⓑ Kim

The stronger the magnet, the more paper clips it can attract at the same time.

Use the table to answer Questions 7 and 8.

Magnet	Number of Paper Clips Attracted
A	7
B	3
C	5

7. Which magnet is the strongest?

   Ⓐ Magnet A

   Ⓑ Magnet B

   Ⓒ Magnet C

8. An even stronger magnet attracts as many paper clips as Magnet A, Magnet B, and Magnet C together. How many paper clips in all does the stronger magnet attract?

   Ⓐ 8

   Ⓑ 10

   Ⓒ 12

   Ⓓ 15

Unit F, Chapter 2

Choose the best answer. Mark the letter for that answer.

Use the pictures below to answer Questions 9 and 10.

9. When you pour water into bottles and then tap the bottles, you hear sounds. The less water there is in the bottle, the higher the pitch of the sound is.

1   2   3   4   5   6

Which bottle will have the highest pitch?

Ⓐ   Bottle 2

Ⓑ   Bottle 4

Ⓒ   Bottle 5

Ⓓ   Bottle 6

10. Which two bottles will have the same pitch?

Ⓐ   Bottles 1 and 3

Ⓑ   Bottles 2 and 3

Ⓒ   Bottles 4 and 5

Ⓓ   Bottles 5 and 6

11. The triangle is a musical instrument.

Kathy tapped a triangle gently and could hear the sound for 2 seconds. Kathy tapped the triangle harder and could hear the sound for 5 seconds. Which number sentence shows how much longer the sound lasted when Kathy hit the triangle harder?

Ⓐ $5 - 2 = 3$

Ⓑ $5 + 3 = 8$

Ⓒ $5 + 2 = 7$

Ⓓ $5 - 1 = 4$

12. Jack did not hear the alarm clock ring at

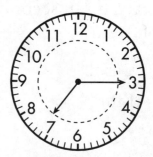

Jack got out of bed when the alarm clock rang again 15 minutes later. What time did Jack get out of bed?

Ⓐ   7:30   Ⓒ   8:00

Ⓑ   7:45   Ⓓ   8:15

Go On

© Harcourt

Unit F, Chapter 2

Choose the best answer. Mark the letter for that answer.

13. Ross made 4 guitars. He used 3 rubber bands for each guitar. How many rubber bands did he use in all?

(A) 8

(B) 10

(C) 12

(D) 14

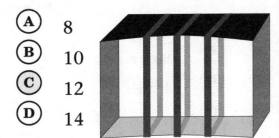

14. The sound from the alarm clock travels through the air to David's ears and wakes him up. What time does the clock show?

(A) 6:00

(B) 6:30

(C) 7:00

(D) 7:30

Use the graph below to answer Questions 15 and 16.

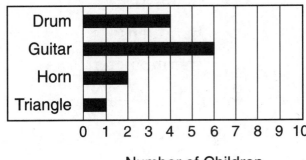

Favorite Musical Instruments

Number of Children

15. Which instrument did **MOST** of the children like best?

(A) drum

(B) guitar

(C) horn

(D) triangle

16. How many children in all chose a favorite instrument?

(A) 6

(B) 10

(C) 12

(D) 13

© Harcourt

Math Practice

Unit F, Review

Choose the best answer. Mark the letter for that answer.

17. Which tool should you use to measure the distance a ball travels?

(A) meterstick

(B) hand lens

(C) thermometer

(D) stopwatch

18. Bob pushed two toy cars. Car A went 30 centimeters. Car B went 55 centimeters. Which car was given a harder push?

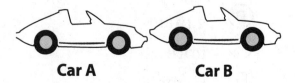

Car A   **Car B**

(A) Car A

(B) Car B

19. Less force is needed to move light objects and more force is needed to move heavy objects. Which object takes the most force to move?

(A) spoon

(B) pan

(C) stove

(D) radio

20. When you pour water into bottles and then tap the bottles, you hear sounds. The more water there is in the bottle, the lower the pitch of the sound is.

Which bottle will have the lowest pitch?

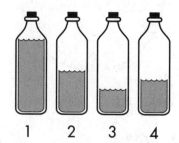

1   2   3   4

(A) Bottle 1

(B) Bottle 2

(C) Bottle 3

(D) Bottle 4

© Harcourt

HARCOURT SCIENCE

PRACTICE FOR STANFORD 9

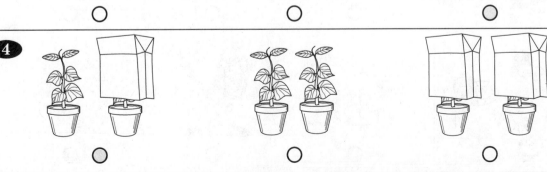

Objectives
1, 2

SAMPLE A

○   ●   ○

SAMPLE B

○   ○   ○

1

Group A | Group B

○   ○   ○

2

Group A | Group B

○   ○   ○

3

FRESH WATER | FRESH WATER   SALT WATER | SALT WATER   SALT WATER | FRESH WATER

○   ○   ○

4

○   ○   ○

© Harcourt

Name _____

1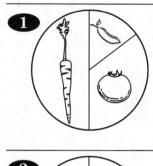

○   ○   ○

2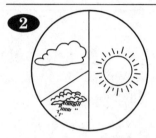

○   ○   ○

3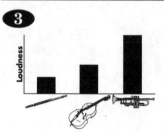

○   ○   ○

4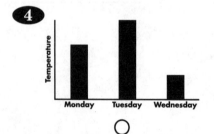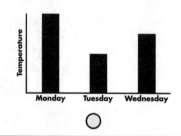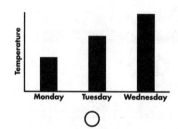

○   ○   ○

5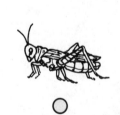

○   ○   ○

6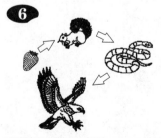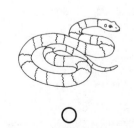

○   ○   ○

© Harcourt

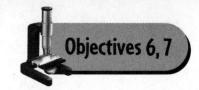

Objectives 6, 7

1

○ ○ ○

2

  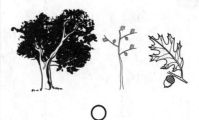

○ ○ ○

3

○ ○ ○

4

○ ○ ○

5

○ ○ ○

6

  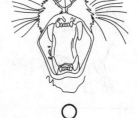

○ ○ ○

© Harcourt

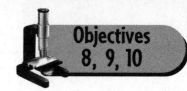

1  |  ◯    ◯

2  | 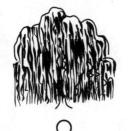 ◯    ◯    ◯

3 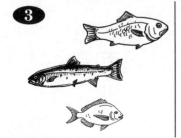 |  ◯   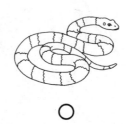 ◯    ◯

4  |  ◯    ◯    ◯

5  ◯    ◯    ◯

6  ◯    ◯    ◯

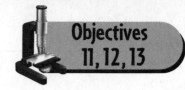

Objectives
11, 12, 13

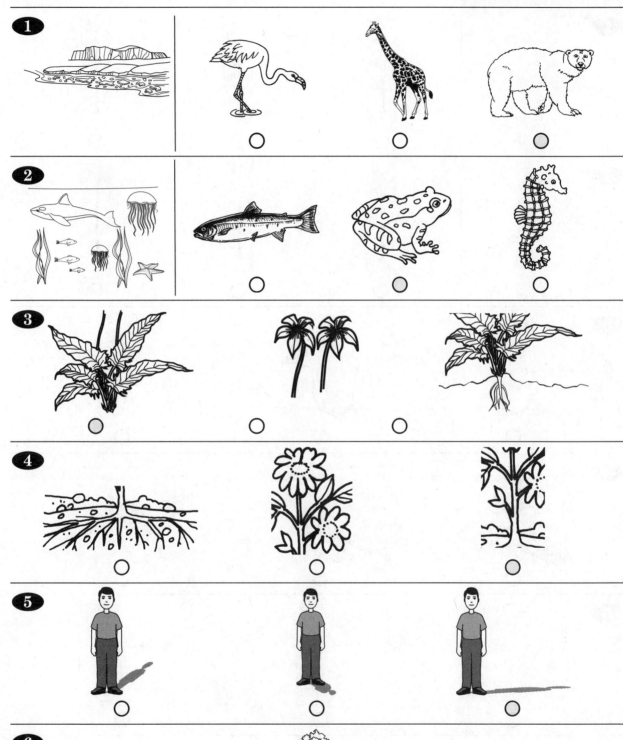

© Harcourt

Objectives 14, 15, 16

1

○   ○   ○

2

○   ○   ○

3

○   ○   ○

4

  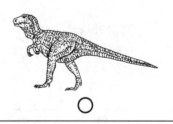

○   ○   ○

5

○   ○   ○

6

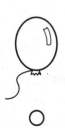  

○   ○   ○

© Harcourt

Name _____

1

   ○

   ○

   ○

2

   ○

   ○

   ○

3

   ○

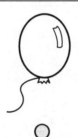   ○

   ○

4

   ○

   ○

   ○

5

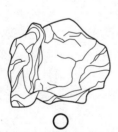   ○

   ○

   ○

6

   ○

   ○

   ○

Name _____

SAMPLE A

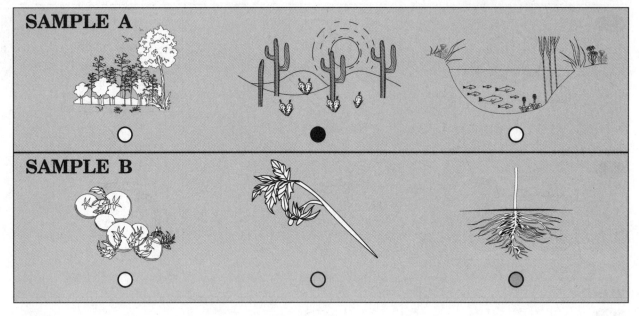

○　　　　　●　　　　　○

SAMPLE B

○　　　　　○　　　　　◍

1

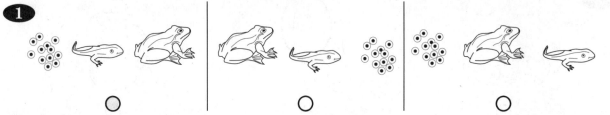

○　　　　　○　　　　　○

2

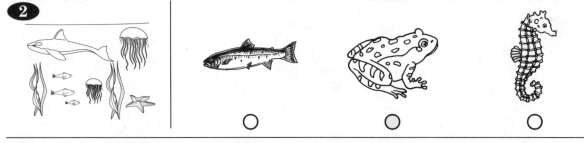

○　　　　　○　　　　　○

3

FRESH WATER　FRESH WATER　　SALT WATER　SALT WATER　　SALT WATER　FRESH WATER

○　　　　　○　　　　　○

4

○　　　　　○　　　　　○

Go On

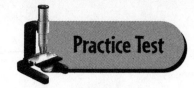

5  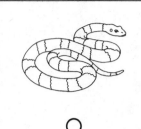 ◯  ◯  ◯

6  ◯  ◯  ◯

7  ◯  ◯ 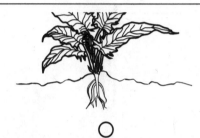 ◯

8  ◯  ◯  ◯

9  ◯ 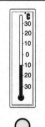 ◯  ◯  ◯

10 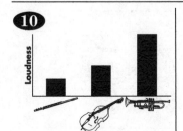 ◯  ◯  ◯

Go On

Practice Test

11

○   ○   ○

12

○   ○   ○

13

○   ○   ○

14

  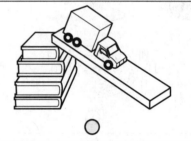

○   ○   ○

15

  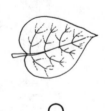 

○   ○   ○

16

○   ○   ○

Go On

© Harcourt

Practice Test

17   ○   ○  ○

18  ○  ○ 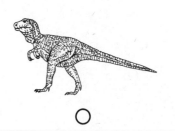 ○

19  ○  ○  ○

20   ○ 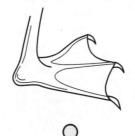 ○  ○

Stop